TO TURN THE TIDE

(AMERICA'S LONGEST-TENURED
UNIVERSITY PRESIDENT MAPS
A RESCUE FOR OUR CRISIS-
CAUGHT INDEPENDENT COLLEGES
AND UNIVERSITIES AND TELLS
WHY WE CANNOT SAY NO.)

by

PAUL C. REINERT S.J.

President, Saint Louis University
1972 Chairman, Association
of American Colleges

Prentice-Hall, Inc., *Englewood Cliffs, N.J.*

ISBN: 0–13–923235–4

Library of Congress Catalog Card Number: 74–39030

10   9   8   7   6   5   4   3   2

Prentice-Hall International, Inc., *London*
Prentice-Hall of Australia, Pty. Ltd., *Sydney*
Prentice-Hall of Canada, Ltd., *Toronto*
Prentice-Hall of India Private Limited, *New Delhi*
Prentice-Hall of Japan, Inc., *Tokyo*

CONTENTS

FOREWORD   v

PREFACE   viii

ACKNOWLEDGMENTS   xi

PROJECT SEARCH   xv

INTRODUCTION   1

part one

    REQUIEM FOR A SYSTEM   13

part two

    PRIVATE HIGHER EDUCATION—WHO NEEDS IT?   25

part three

    COLLEGE FINANCE: HOW MUCH, FOR WHAT, FROM WHOM?   40

part four

    RESCUE BEGINS AT HOME—THE CAMPUS IMPERATIVES   54

CONTENTS

part five

THE STATE'S ROLE—TO LEAD THE WAY   71

part six

FEDERAL AID—IMMEDIACY THE KEY   86

part seven

WHERE TO FROM HERE?   103

ABOUT THE AUTHOR   109

FOREWORD

Thoughtful men who have pondered the sources which nurture a democratic society never fail to agree on at least one: a potent system of higher education. But there is much diversity of opinion on the best means of supporting such a system.

The author of this enlightened book is deeply convinced that the problem must be approached pluralistically, that whatever happens to our independent colleges and universities, good or bad, will affect our public institutions as well.

Obviously a weakening of independent private institutions would open the way for a higher education system totally a creature of government, with all the potential for intrusion and control this implies. Healthy independent institutions provide an alternative, a haven where intellectual non-conformity has equal house, where scholars can be at odds with the prevailing doctrine within a framework of tolerance and objectivity. Our dual system of education—public and private—assures this diversity.

This is the context in which the longest-tenured university president in our land, Paul Reinert, sounds his clarion call—*To Turn the Tide*. He defines a threat to our present educational system that is serious but little recognized beyond education circles. The financial crisis that now menaces our independent colleges and universities is too often blandly assumed to be not a fight for survival, but simply a shakeout, a purification process in which outmoded and inefficient programs will be shed, leaving the rejuvenated institutions to live happily ever after. Would that it were so. Father Reinert cuts through this illusion and draws the issue sharply as a matter of stark survival. Indeed, for some colleges and universities the end is alarmingly near—after nearly two generations of rampant inflation. Yet, as he discloses in these pages, threatened institutions tend to minimize the desperateness of their situations for fear of weakening morale and support when they can least afford to do so.

Private education stands today at the cross-roads of renewal or collapse. Decimation of our independent colleges and universities would have the most serious repercussions—educational, social, cultural, and political. It is imperative that more dollars be found not merely to support those institutions but to strengthen them.

Toward that end, the United States Congress is attempting to fashion a legislative solution. Whether it will suffice, and whether adequate financial support will be made available by the Administration, remains to be seen. In any case, support from foundations, business, industry and individuals is equally necessary if private education as we have known it is to survive.

Pragmatist that he is, Father Reinert faces the situation squarely, candidly. Writing with the clear perspective of one who has been through it all, he tells why the patient is ill, why it is worth saving, and how it can be saved. He deals directly with the familiar charge that inefficiency and poor business practices have brought on the malady. He disagrees with those who hold that the distinction between public and private institutions is blurred and that private institutions have therefore become expendable. He deals with the issue of public funds to support private education, and the principle of separation of church and state in the use of tax money for education. He comments persuasively on the obligation of the state to its residents to help maintain our traditional dual public-and-private system of higher education—and tells how this should be done. He reports in some detail the story behind the new Congressional "rescue measures," a story that should interest legislators as well as educators throughout the nation.

Most important of all, Father Reinert blueprints the efforts that are required from government, from the public and from higher education itself. In sum, this remarkable book presents all that is important for one to know about our current crisis in American higher education. For parent and politician, instructor and industrialist, philanthropist and philosopher, scientist and stevedore—for everyone who cares whether school keeps—Father Reinert provides a practical, sensible program for action.

FRANK STANTON

Vice-Chairman
Columbia Broadcasting
System

PREFACE

"Speak to us smooth things, prophesy illusions," said the people in Isaiah's time. And so say many in our time—some legislators, some businessmen, some alumni, even some administrators in private institutions of higher learning—about the problems of private higher education. "Perhaps," they say, "it is better than it seems and wishing can make it so. Prophesy illusions."

Paul Reinert has not let his ear be tickled by this plea. Before the second half of this volume—the proposed remedies—can make much sense, the severity of the problem must first be clearly articulated. This is the serious task assigned to the first half of the book.

Nearly half of America's private accredited colleges and universities—as we have pointed out elsewhere—could be on the verge of bankruptcy within the decade as the consequence of having exhausted their total liquid assets. Father Reinert, appalled that this could be happening without most people being aware of it, insists that the situation—delicate and precarious as it may be—be faced with courage, candor, and honesty.

Pointing out the seriousness of the situation triggers a nervous reaction in some anxious administrators in private institutions. Pointing it out, they fear, may help bring it about. A soft voice and sweet reason may be all that is needed. True enough. But, as the man who took a two-by-four to the back of the Missouri mule said, "First you have to get his attention."

Private higher education may be facing its last hurrah unless the severity of its financial plight is realized and understood—and unless all those in a position to respond do so swiftly. Like Dickens' Ghost of Christmas Future, Father Reinert is concerned to show what might be.

He gives expression to the critical nature of the situation in order to summon attentive concern for the practical remedies he sets forth. These are designed to carry us through debate to action; for the question of private higher education's survival is no longer academic.

For those who have lost sight of the compelling importance of private institutions for our society, Father Reinert makes a fresh statement of the case. Their importance lies not simply in what they have produced in the past or what they contribute in the present, but in the safeguard they provide for the future. Constitutional freedoms—including freedom of religion—may not be very meaningful if the institutions that give expression to those freedoms do not possess the means to exist. Also, the continuance of private institutions of higher learning provides assurance of academic freedom for both our public and private sectors.

Private higher education is caught between two abrasive forces: those that permit too little and those that expect too much. Those that require conformity and those that expect uniqueness. Pressed on the one side by forces compelling commonness—including the slivered edges of wooden interpretations of the first amendment—private higher education is rubbed raw on the other by those who seem to believe both that it is possible to be at once impoverished and unique, and necessary that an institution be literally one-of-a-kind in order to justify its existence.

Private higher education needs to be perceived as qualitatively different—but hardly as unique—in order to survive. It is for this reason that its present plight is more serious than that of tax-supported institutions. For a tax-supported institution to decline in prestige is grievous but not catastrophic. Its survival is not apt to be at stake. However, if a private institution undergoes a corresponding loss of prestige its survival may be in real doubt.

The remedies Father Reinert proposes—at the institutional, state, and federal levels—are pragmatic and immediate. His recommendations for setting each institution's house in order are wise and workable. Private higher education, like its public counterpart, needs both to be accountable and to perform in such a way as to be unashamed in its statement of accountability.

After private sources, Father Reinert argues, the primary responsibility of government for the support of private higher education rests with the state. It is important that the federal government demonstrate its support for the private sector and important that federal and state aid mesh together; but for economic and bureaucratic reasons, the state must be the larger contributor to the financial health of the private college and university.

The chapters on state and federal programs are very helpful analyses of the kinds of aid most likely to be useful and most able to work well in conjunction with one another. The arguments for loans to students related to later income are more persuasive to me than they appear to be to Father Reinert, but he is wise to resist them as the single financial answer.

No one whose attention has been captured by the problem will come away from these last chapters without being offered concrete proposals for remedy. The question now is: Can we get action while there is still time?

WILLIAM W. JELLEMA

ACKNOWLEDGMENTS

I wish to thank all those whose cooperation, encouragement, and thinking enabled me to pursue Project SEARCH and ultimately to produce this manuscript.

I especially want to thank Joseph P. Cosand, Deputy Commissioner of Higher Education, U.S. Office of Education, and Willis M. Tate, President of Southern Methodist University, who, as Chairmen of the American Council on Education and of the Association of American Colleges respectively, aided me in initiating this project.

My gratitude also goes to Clark Kerr and his staff at the Carnegie Commission on Higher Education for their generous cooperation and for making available research data and tentative drafts of forthcoming publications.

I appreciate the help given by those who granted personal interviews and participated in our SEARCH conferences.

I am also grateful to the Danforth Foundation for its generosity and confidence shown in awarding me the grant to make possible the Project SEARCH effort. Finally, my gratitude goes to Fred Gehrung for help with the preparation of this manuscript and with every phase of Project SEARCH.

PAUL C. REINERT S.J.

Partial List of Persons Consulted in Project SEARCH

Joseph M. Bertotti
Manager, Educational Relations
General Electric Co.

Howard R. Bowen
Chancellor
Claremont University Center

Rep. John Brademas (Dem.-Ind.)

Paul Brinkley-Rogers
Los Angeles Bureau
Newsweek

Vincent C. Burke, Jr.
Executive Vice President
Riggs National Bank, Washington,
D.C.

Allan Cartter
Chancellor
New York University

James Cass
Education Editor
Saturday Review

Earl Cheit
Professor of Business Administration
University of California

Joseph P. Cosand
Deputy Commissioner of Higher
Education
U.S. Office of Education

Fred E. Crossland
Program Officer
The Ford Foundation

Michael Curtis
Associate Editor
Atlantic Monthly

True Davis
President and Chairman of the Board
National Bank of Washington

Walter G. Davis
Director, Department of Education
AFL-CIO

Philip H. Des Marais
Director, Office of Research Services
Fordham University

William H. Dodds
Director, Citizenship Department
United Auto Workers

Sen. Thomas Eagleton (Dem-Mo.)

Mel Elfin
Washington Bureau
Newsweek

Lloyd Elliot
President
George Washington University

Alvin C. Eurich
President
Academy for Educational Development

Richard C. Gilman
President
Occidental College

Rep. Edith Green (Dem.-Ore.)

Fred Hechinger
New York Times

Harry Hogan
Legislative Counsel
Office of Rep. Edith Green

Harold Howe
Vice President, Division of Education
  and Research
The Ford Foundation

William W. Jellema
Executive Associate and Research
  Director
Association of American Colleges

L. A. Jennings
Chairman of the Board
Riggs National Bank, Washington,
  D.C.

Joseph Kane
Associate Director
Association of Jesuit Colleges and
  Universities

Sen. Edward M. Kennedy
  (Dem.-Mass.)

Francis C. Keppel
President
General Learning Corp.

Clark Kerr
Chairman
Carnegie Commission on Higher
  Education

Don H. McGannon
President
Westinghouse Broadcasting Co., Inc.

Sidney P. Marland
U.S. Commissioner of Education

Warren B. Martin
Center for Research and Develop-
  ment in Higher Education
University of California

Curt Matthews
Washington Bureau
St. Louis Post-Dispatch

John F. Morse
Director, Commission on Federal
  Relations
American Council on Education

Sidney Mudd
President
New York Seven-Up Bottling Co.

Peter P. Muirhead
Executive Deputy Commissioner
U.S. Office of Education

Franklin D. Murphy, M.D.
Chairman of the Board
Times-Mirror Co.

Alfred Neal
President
Committee for Economic Develop-
  ment

Frederic W. Ness
President
Association of American Colleges

Frank Newman
Chairman
Task Force on Higher Education

Morgan Odell
Executive Director
Association of Independent California
  Colleges and Universities

Eugene Patterson
Managing Editor
Washington Post

Sen. Claiborne Pell (Dem.-R.I.)

Rep. Albert Quie (Rep.-Minn.)

Sen. Richard Schweiker (Rep.-Penn.)

Joseph T. Shutt
Vice President
Council for Financial Aid to Educa-
  tion, Inc.

Elden T. Smith
Executive Secretary
National Council of Independent
  Colleges and Universities

G. Kerry Smith
Former Chief Executive Officer
American Association of Higher
  Education

Virginia B. Smith
Assistant Director
Carnegie Commission on Higher
  Education

Rep. William A. Steiger (Rep.-Wis.)

Richard Sullivan
Assistant to the President
Carnegie Foundation

Sen. Stuart Symington (Dem.-Mo.)

William H. Taft
Office of Management and Budget

Willis Tate
President, Southern Methodist
  University

E. E. Trefethen, Jr.
President
Kaiser Industries

William Trombley
Education Editor
Los Angeles Times

Clarence Walton
President
Catholic University of America

Robert J. Wert
President
Mills College

Edward Bennett Williams
Attorney at Law

Logan Wilson
Former President
American Council on Education

John D. Young
Chief
Economic, Science and Technology
  Division
U.S. Office of Management and
  Budget

Kenneth Young
Assistant Director
Department of Legislation
AFL-CIO

PROJECT SEARCH

SEARCH was a national effort, the format of which was a conference series directed by the Reverend Paul C. Reinert, S.J., president of Saint Louis University and chairman of the Association of American Colleges, to conceive a course of action that will (1) solve the financial dilemma of private higher education and (2) achieve the strong, pluralistic public/private higher education system that is best and least costly for our nation.

While SEARCH was a mission to rescue and to restore private higher education to sound footing, the interrelationship with the public sector is such that any success achieved would be shared by both and greatly profit our national educational system overall.

Thus the nature of the need and of the task is not alone the concern of any one sector of education or government or of the public, but the vested interest of all. And likewise, the responses to and the sanctions for SEARCH came not alone from any single sector but from a diversity of leaders and organizations across the country.

The conference series as the medium for SEARCH was precisely suited to the project intent, which was to achieve a synthesis of the thinking of leaders within education, government, business, labor, communications and other widely diverse fields. Heretofore, concern over the problem has, for the most part, brought examination by given sectors within the context of the particular field, e.g., business leaders approaching it as a business matter. The SEARCH conferences brought about the desired interchanges of thinking and expertise—the intellectual critical mass—expected to yield the sought-for solutions and their implementation.

As project director, Father Reinert's mission was to start where various reports and studies made to date left off and to come forward with the action that must be taken to accomplish the previously stated aims. Essentially, the undertaking made use of such important findings as those of the Carnegie Commission on Higher Education as the point from which to proceed.

The key questions posed were these: (1) What are the essential needs for survival of private education? (2) What can be done practically to have these essentials implemented immediately?

INTRODUCTION

We all know that higher education in our land must change drastically, but a major sector of the American system of higher education will not be around to change unless some short-range —in fact immediate—measures are adopted for its rescue and renewal.

The sector in imminent danger of collapse is our private one—the 1,500 independent colleges and universities currently educating one out of every four of the young men and women on our campuses. The threat: bankruptcy. The malaise of fiscal deterioration infecting these institutions may weaken them to the point of no return.

What is appalling to me as the president of one such institution is that this can happen without most people consciously aware that it is happening. As this financial malady has progressed from a remote danger to a real and fast-spreading illness, more and more independent colleges and universities have slid toward various types of oblivion—some closing down, some merging, some being absorbed into public systems, some only half-alive and serving so small a percentage of the population so poorly that it may be merciful to put them out of their unhappy, unfruitful existence.

To halt this slide, federal and state legislators, political lead-ers, media opinion-makers, and professional, business, and labor leaders must join with educators to convince the American public that we would be forfeiting one of the nation's greatest assets— the pluralistic system of higher education with its balance of public and independent institutions. For it to be saved, Ameri-cans must recognize and acknowledge the desirability and the need for doing so.

Then general guidelines must be agreed to for the adequate support of these deficit-ridden schools. Next we must strive to win legal, moral, and public acceptance of these guidelines. That such an effort can prevail seems plausible based upon these as-sumptions set forth in Howard Bowen's *The Finance of Higher Education*:

1. The United States should maintain an excellent system of higher education, affording rich opportunities for the per-sonal development of its young people and giving high na-tional priority to the advancement of learning.
2. This system should be diversified (a) as to *program* so as to meet the needs of students of various backgrounds; (b) as to *control* so as to achieve the healthy academic independence provided by having both private and public institutions; (c) as to *sources of support* so that no interest group can dominate higher education.
3. Higher education should be available to all with no limitation other than capacity and desire; hence with no barriers of finance, race, religion, place of residence, or academic back-ground.
4. Students should have free choice of educational programs and institutions within the limits of their qualifications.

If you accept these assumptions, as I believe most Americans do, the questions to be answered include (1) What should be the priorities and the methods of funding higher education, especially the private sector? (2) How should this funding be borne by the student, his family, by other private sources, by the state and the Federal governments? (3) How can these priorities and their ap-propriate funding be implemented before it is too late? Put differently, what are the minimal essential support programs necessary to buy time for the survival of our independent colleges and universities until long-range recommendations and legislation can have an effect?

The Mission Defined

It was to these questions that Project SEARCH addressed itself. Our intention was to conceive just such a strategy—practical immediate action to be taken at both the institutional and governmental level. We viewed the task as part rescue mission and part holding action—an undertaking of urgency and importance to the public as well as the private sectors of higher education. For the weakening and closing of independent colleges and universities gravely affects the stability of public institutions, themselves beginning to suffer deficits and tremble beneath overburdening enrollments.

The demise of private colleges and universities would only force the state public systems into more costly and unnecessary expansions. Thus while Project SEARCH was undertaken to restore private higher education, its interrelationship with the public sector is such that any success achieved would profit the national system overall. For this reason, the responses to and the sanctions for our project came not from any single sector of society alone but from a diversity of interests and organizations across the country.

Project SEARCH, funded by the Danforth Foundation, took the form of a national conference series, a medium precisely suiting our intention of bringing to bear and synthesizing the thinking of leaders in education, government, business, labor communications, and other fields. Heretofore, concern for this problem had, for the most part, inspired independent examination by given sectors which tended to explore approaches and remedies within the context of their individual fields—for example, business leaders approaching it as a business matter.

Through Project SEARCH, we sought a solution generated

by interchanges among the fields that would deal with all aspects of the problem—financial as well as operational. What I was after didn't exist in studies or reports but in the minds of the conference participants. I wanted the different points of view. These I got, and this was what was so worthwhile and unique about our project—the opportunity for such a dialogue. It was quite different from educators talking to educators, businessmen talking to businessmen.

The experience left me with one encouraging and three disturbing impressions. I was disturbed first by the deep-set doubt and misgivings about higher education in general, and especially private higher education. There was serious questioning of the existence of any *real* difference between private and public institutions, about whether the nation could justify the expense and effort of maintaining the private sector. It was clear that our conference participants had been looking, but largely in vain, for distinctive programs on the private campuses.

Second, there was a propensity to support rather simplistic solutions—for example, if the independent colleges would only apply sound business principles, or if we would abandon the tenure system, or if the faculty would teach more hours, the problem would take care of itself.

The third point that came home to me was the realization that geographic location can possibly be the greatest single deterrent to survival of a private institution today. For example, all other things being equal, a college across the river from Saint Louis University in Illinois has a much better chance to weather the current financial crisis than we do in the state of Missouri; while Illinois has a strong program of state assistance, Missouri has none at all.

On the positive side, it was made clear that at the Federal level—in the Senate, the House, and on the part of the Administration—the question has changed from *whether* to aid the private institutions to one of *how* best to help. Talking with Senators and Congressmen at work on legislation to provide such assistance was most encouraging.

What follows on these pages is the result of such talks—the

culmination of the Project SEARCH deliberations. Our starting point was where various excellent reports and studies made to date left off. Our hope: to come forward from there with a recommended course of action.

The Several Horns of the Dilemma

Probably no aspect of American society has been more the target of such dedicated, scholarly, expert study or more heavily researched or examined by individuals, commissions, and agencies at considerable expense and effort than has higher education. Various foundations have rendered invaluable service in this regard. My prayer is that we can make the most of it, but to do so, ways need to be found to keep the patient alive long enough for treatment to be administered and take effect—long enough for reform and renewal, long enough to bring about a rededication of the American public to our pluralistic higher education system which, albeit imperfect, has served our citizenry well and helped preserve us as a free nation under God.

In discussions throughout the SEARCH conferences, Congressmen, business leaders, and others said that it was difficult to get an accurate fix on many aspects of the problem. They complained that supportive financial data seemed inexact and incomplete. For this reason some of these persons questioned whether the crisis was indeed more than a healthy adjustment overdue within higher education. So that any readers with similar thoughts may have a proper perspective, two points made during the SEARCH meetings bear repeating here:

1. Scientific, reliable unit cost analysis, like academic innovation and compensatory programs for disadvantaged students, is extremely expensive. Though this does not argue that such analysis should not be done, it does explain why fiscally threatened colleges have been slow to add this cost to their overburdened budgets.
2. Just as the federal government struggles with the balancing of two obligations—disclosure of information the citizenry has

a right to know and nondisclosure of information that might jeopardize national security—so, too, does the independent college walk the narrow line between telling the public, including the government, what the seriousness of its plight is and disclosing data that could crush morale and send faculty, students, and donors elsewhere. How much can be told to the public?

Thus college and university presidents, aware that intoning disaster can become a self-fulfilling prophecy, are extremely reluctant to tell it like it is. Those in the deepest trouble are inclined to say the least. So delicate and precarious a situation requires courage and honesty on the part of higher education and understanding and discretion on the part of governmental officials and various fact-finding groups.

The outlook? For many schools to break even at the present rate of inflation, their income will have to grow at the rate of 6.5 percent per student per year, according to Dr. Earl F. Cheit's widely read book, *The New Depression in Higher Education.* At the same time he projects that income cannot be expected to grow as much as 5 percent per student per year. That is the outlook— red as in ink and redder as in bankruptcy.

No, tomorrow isn't promised to anybody, and no one is more aware of this than the presidents of our independent colleges and universities. Today's new college president finds that his first job is to scale *down* the school's plans, to trim the operations of his predecessor who probably fell victim to his own grand design. The talk is of retrenchment, reallocating, hanging on—survival.

Yet while surviving, the school must enrich itself, be contemporary, satisfy a new breed of customer—today's student arrives with an ever lower boredom threshold and ever higher expectations of the institution, its program and faculty—the school being "on probation" until it proves itself "worthy," one might say.

Today, many presidents of private colleges or universities (and an increasing number of public institutions as well) endure the everyday reality of impending financial breakdown. Their problems would be a nightmare to any industry plant manager.

The scene often is at once intense, frustrating, and pressured, with administrators yoked to problems whose solutions are in part out of their hands.

This is university administration today, a condition of the job and the milieu within which innovation and renewal must be spawned. I speak of this from deep personal involvement, having perhaps the longest tenure as a university president in the land. Unlike the members of many task forces or research staffs or committees of various organizations taking a look at this dilemma, I have been and am on the firing line, experiencing personally the trauma of an institution threatened with economic strangulation.

Granted I hold a particular viewpoint and this entails a disadvantage, but then perhaps I can help counterbalance the over-generalized, theoretical, leisurely, and detached approaches of some diagnosticians who have not personally been pushed to the wall in the daily bloody fiscal encounters characterizing what Cheit terms our "higher education depression." Because the nature of commissions and task forces diagnosing our illness is necessarily general and they deal with total higher education, the private sector and peculiarities of its problem are not paid adequate separate attention. If we within this sector do not speak out for ourselves, no one else will. For this reason, Project SEARCH served an additional need as a forum from which to articulate and emphasize both the value and the imperilment of private higher education.

At the same time, I personally hoped that through Project SEARCH I could clarify my own thinking as to what were the two or three immediate things that ought to be done. For this was not a case of my campaigning for a strategy that I had up my sleeve. I had no plan for the salvation of private higher education to promulgate—though I wished that I had, particularly when some conference participant would say, "Why not begin by telling us your plan?" or when some Congressman would ask, "What is it you want us to do?" But this is why our endeavor was called SEARCH. We were seeking such answers. We hoped to determine what could be done *now*. This, as you will see on the following pages, we seem to have achieved. For the project did indeed fine-tune my perspective and suggest a three-dimensional strategy with the following imperatives at the academic, state, and Federal levels.

The Broad Conclusions of SEARCH

1. The academic community must put its own house in order by balancing its budget, improving its management and planning, making more effective use of resources, conceiving new and stimulating approaches and programs, and defining its aims and sticking to them alone.

2. The state governments must provide or expand two or three basic programs that will achieve a strong public/private balance for higher education and a uniform level of assistance among all states.

3. The Federal government must provide or enlarge two or three basic programs that will render immediate aid to faltering institutions, expand higher education opportunities, and create an incentive to do a better job for states lagging in meeting their responsibilities.

It may be useful at this point to outline the overall plan of the volume. There are seven parts as follows:

Part I is largely for readers outside education and briefly describes how the current financial crisis came to pass. This section also treats the many-faceted nature of the problem and the effect that it is having upon not only the private sector but the public one as well.

Part II asks the question, Do we really want our private sector? Both the philosophical and the practical aspects of this question are taken up. Consideration is given to the criticisms leveled at the independent schools—for example, that they have lost their distinctiveness—as well as to the values that these institutions would seem to hold out to their students, to higher education overall (a safeguard of academic freedom), and to society. The case is made for saving the patient.

Part III describes in general the types of government aid that have been rendered to higher education and their various purposes and results. The objectives that aid should have are specified as (1) to sustain and improve deserving schools, and (2) to achieve greater equality of access. The importance of diversity of support to assure that no one interest group can ever take control is also discussed.

Part IV blueprints what the schools must do to get their own houses in order and points out that while these are the worst of times for the private sector, they could be the best of times for reforms and renewal. At the same time, cautions are issued against short-sighted cutbacks. It is emphasized that a university is not a business and that efficiency is not all-important, though cost accounting and other business practices must be followed. Accountability also is taken up and deemed fair. Church-related institutions are warned against giving up their identity to win government funds, and the important constitutionality issue involving the use of public taxes to support private institutions is covered. The position is taken that church-related colleges and universities can stand for something, be committed, while they provide good secular education and qualify for government aid.

Part V focuses on state aid with the view that the states should maintain their historic central role of responsibility for higher education within their boundaries. The types of state programs are covered with particular attention to the unevenness of aid provided from state to state. Further consideration is given to the constitutionality of government financial aid, this time within the state context. A state tuition equalization program is called for in states that have been lagging. It is pointed out that taxpayers in those states are sustaining the increased financial burden of expanding overcrowded public institutions while the private schools stand by with empty space, not just willing but needing to help.

Part VI deals with Federal aid and where it fits vis-à-vis state and private assistance. A public statement of Federal support for the private sector of higher education is called for and the role that the Federal government should assume is cast as having three aspects: (1) to clearly endorse the pluralistic system; (2) to complement the state aid efforts; and (3) to provide a form of incentive that will stimulate the more sluggish states to meet their responsibility. Specific ways of fulfilling these three purposes are given. Next the House and Senate bills proposed in 1971 for aid to higher education are examined and evaluated and a definite position is taken on each. Importantly, precise arguments are presented for and against various aspects of the proposals together with substitute recommendations.

Part VII is devoted largely to marshaling the many nongovernmental segments of the academic community situated in Washington to speak with a unified voice on those key issues affecting overall higher education. Steps toward such an alliance of organizations are given. It is suggested that only by uniting can the sundry increments of private higher education's Washington presence ever form a compelling enough entity to win for it a deserved high ranking among national priorities.

―――――

The reader will notice some seeming repetition or overlap in the treatment of certain issues. This is because there are factors or arguments that have application in more than one section. Some of the elements with which we are concerned are relevant to more than one topic—for example, the constitutionality matter is taken up as an influence upon the much-criticized lessening of distinctiveness among our colleges and universities and also figures importantly in a subsequent section on state aid. It is felt that such handling is useful and appropriate in order to best treat the subject.

Also worth calling the reader's attention to is the element of fluidity involved where the status of the Federal legislation treated herein is concerned. It is remotely possible that the Senate and House, currently awaiting reconciliation of their two proposed bills will have reached a compromise and even passed a higher education aid measure by the time this volume is published. It will then become a question of whether or not the funds are made available—thus what is said in our section on the necessity for Federal aid becomes all the more germane.

To conclude, this effort was not undertaken as one more offering of or for the academic community nor as one more assessment or cry for help, but as a suggested map through the tunnel and also as a story that badly needs telling to our citizenry. This includes parents and students who deserve to know the penalty they would have to pay in (1) loss of the options offered under a public/private, two-sector form of higher education, (2) degradation of educational quality, or (3) outlandish tuition costs unless we achieve a public-supported collaboration of higher education with the state and Federal governments to turn the tide.

Without such a joint effort and such accord we face the erosion and eventual loss of our pluralistic system—a national asset that would be sorely missed and strangely absent from our democracy. For minus the alternative of a private sector, higher education as a bastion of freedom becomes an empty fortress.

REQUIEM FOR A SYSTEM

The campus is still. Empty. Like any corpse, that of a college is not pleasant to behold. Yesterday it was very much alive—what can be more alive, after all, than a college or university? Halls full of laughter, footsteps, hellos. Classrooms full of purpose, ideas, optimism. Dormitories charged with that special wattage of the young. Just yesterday, there flourished here the icon of contemporary American higher education—a college devoted to academic excellence, committed to academic freedom, a total institution for learning, its alumni useful to society. Just yesterday this school with its student body, its faculty, and its administrators made for plenty of life. But today it is over. The final bell has sounded. And administrators of independent colleges and universities like this one throughout the land will not send to know for whom the bell tolls. They know that it tolls for them.

Many of these same administrators have come from around the country to attend the auction—no, the wake—and they stand fidgeting as final rites are performed, three classrooms at a time, by an auctioneer. The litany: "What am I bid?"

The college stands on the crest of a hill, the buildings deep red brick with the wood trim gleaming white —freshly painted. Inside, in the classrooms, books still lie on the desks, chalk and erasers wait at the blackboards, maps and charts hang on the walls. Down an empty corridor, the president's office, unopened mail on the big mahogany desk. Further on, the library, quieter now than libraries are meant to be. It is as if a bell has rung and everyone has filed out. Perhaps for a fire drill.

This is what remains after the president of a college or university calls the faculty together and announces that the bills can no longer be paid, that you're getting your last paycheck . . . that he's very sorry. You grab your coat and run out. It will hit you later like a hammer. But right now you have to land a job. Left behind, papers unmarked in a drawer, a lesson chalked on the board . . . for no one.

And then the auction. And it's over. No chit-chat. Participants are as reluctant to speak, as they were to bid. For all present are much more affected by what has come to pass than by the bargain. A college has died, and they are here to carry things away.

No one will say it can't happen to my school. These administrators of the nation's independent colleges and universities know better. They know that it is a tricky business, spending more than you take in and getting by with it . . . until tomorrow. In a word association test, a layman's response to "college" might be "education"; but to most independent college or university presidents, the answer would be "deficit." . . . writ large. And for this particular mid-America

increases upon the public sector to accommodate a still greater flow of students through already brimming conduits and to seek more funds from state legislatures ever less willing to spend more tax dollars in this area.

According to a survey by the National Association of State Universities and Land-Grant Colleges, the first public-supported university to operate at a deficit was Nebraska in 1967. In 1969 the figure rose to five; by 1970 there were a dozen. Public universities anticipating a deficit in 1971 are Alabama A & M, Florida State, Oklahoma State, Rutgers, Houston, Michigan, Maine, Alaska, and Vermont. In many states, public institutions are prevented by law from operating at a deficit, or the list would be longer. Pennsylvania State University is reported to have borrowed $85.5 million from private sources and the University of South Carolina is said to be borrowing from its unrestricted endowment principal. Other major state universities in deepening financial troubles are Missouri, Minnesota, Wisconsin, and California (Berkeley).

Boom Builds to a Bust

As all of us in public and private higher education know too well too late, the pox that has befallen both our houses consists largely of uncontrollable developments whose dire effects could c been lessened had we managed our households differently. To recount briefly for those readers less familiar with what has transpired . . .

In the beginning—meaning the early 1960s—our educational system experienced record growth. To meet the anticipated onsweep of students, the emphasis was on building facilities, adding and expanding departments, increasing services, and tackling new programs. Important steps were taken toward correcting inequality of opportunity. Access to college broadened. Higher academe boomed, the investment in physical plants soaring toward the estimated $38 billion that it is today (with an annual operating cost of about $14 billion).

But the flood of students proved to be something less than

a blessing. It weakened rather than strengthened the condition of our colleges and universities by rendering them more vulnerable to subsequent heavy seas. When the economic storm winds crested in 1968–1969 and these institutions needed to be at their soundest, they were overextended.

Strongest of these winds was inflation, having its most immediate and debilitating effect where it hurt most—salaries, the largest item in a college budget. The salary increase rate then at 5 to 7 percent a year was canceled out by a cost-of-living price rise of 6 percent. At the same time, cost of construction and maintenance of facilities soared—doubling between 1966 and 1970. Up went the cost of libraries, library equipment, scientific apparatus, and computer services that have to be continually purchased to stay abreast of the knowledge explosion and to meet modern operating demands.

While inflation was eroding the underpinnings, the schools were busily overcommitting themselves, responding to increased demands for research help, for wider services, for expanded access, and for socially current programs, as Earl Cheit recounts in *The New Depression in Higher Education.*

Then came the crunch: an economic slump that presented us with the worst of two worlds—recession *and* inflation (at least during the '30s, prices fell along with income). For independent colleges and universities, the slowdown and accompanying stock market thrombosis brought these convulsions: less corporate funds available for gifts; a diminishing of the tax incentive that encourages private donation of stocks when stock prices are rising; a lessening of equity as securities held by the institutions devalued; a dwindling of foundation grant programs because of depressed stock prices.

In response, most schools cut back first on new programs—any innovative enterprises of an experimental nature—bringing up a psychological aspect of both college finance and student enrollment. As many administrators have observed, donors like to give to new and interesting projects and progressing institutions, not simply to help a sagging college get out of the red. And students like to attend vigorous, exciting institutions, not those who are retrenching and narrowing their progrms. However, little that is new and exciting is spawned in red ink. It takes a surplus at year's end to support the sort of innovation that has characterized independent colleges and universities until now. States Jellema, "An institution barely afloat, with water nearly over the gunwales, has lost much of its maneuverability, its adventurousness and freedom of experimentation. Its innovativeness and risk taking is confined to putting to sea each academic year. Most ominously, it has no protection against storms. A little student unrest, a little decline in enrollment, a little disenchantment among donors and the ship may founder."

Private giving also thinned out with the multiplying of priorities and as a reaction to campus unrest, though the latter also is a convenient dodge for contributors feeling the economic pinch. Parenthetically, it is questionable whether even after the economic recovery the relationship between the business sector and independent higher education ever will be what it once was. As the private schools graduate fewer and fewer, business executives come more often from the ranks of state school graduates. More and more management is turning to these institutions for what it once sought from independent colleges and universities.

Meanwhile, back at the Capitol, Federal policy called for a reduction in certain spending—such as aid to education—to battle the inflationary spiral. Which was a 20–20 reading of the taxpayer's frame of mind for three reasons: (1) he was hurting badly himself; (2) he saw other urgent needs for government support programs; (3) he was not happy with alma maters of the land over their seeming inadequacies in dealing with everything from budgets to student disturbances to the quality of education to the price tag on that education.

As a sign of the times and of what has happened to the image of higher education, the president of a newly dedicated public college in New Jersey remarked that it had been very difficult to find a community that wanted a college as a neighbor. He reported looking at more than thirty locations, and that some even passed petitions to keep out the school. All of which contrasted sharply with what he found when starting a college in

Michigan ten years ago when twenty communities begged for the school.

Among fast-escalating costs for independent schools was recruitment, now estimated at as much as $500 per student on the average, compared to $250 in 1967. Included are the higher recruiter salaries and their increased expenses, the school's follow-up activity—for example, phoning, brochures, and entertaining of visitors. The cost of fund-raising has climbed similarly.

The Tuition Dilemma

Ironically, the only thing rising that may hit a ceiling shortly (or in some cases already has) is tuition. So we face a condition in which income is limited and outgo continues rocketing upward. Yet as William Jellema has computed in *The Red and the Black,* if the present trend continues, the average tuition charge at typical independent universities by 1985 will be $17,324 per year (which is less than half of what the average cost to the institution will be for educating the student for one year: $36,859).

Tuition at our independent colleges and universities has been rising at about 7.5 percent per year. But it is far below what it would need to be if it were to pay the entire cost of educating the student. At best, it may now pay 75 percent, but in most cases, it is closer to 50 percent. At any rate, as tuition climbs, an ever smaller number of families can afford to pay it. Thus they reduce educational goals for their youngsters. As the vacancies increase, the tuition must be raised again and the knot tightens.

Upward pressure on tuition among private colleges and universities has also been intensified by aid these schools have extended to the needy, a situation to be discussed in greater detail further on. The Jellema report explains that "as schools move to demonstrate their social concern by extending scholarship money to those unable to pay, they are forced to raise their fees. The result is a new group of students who now require subsidy for the difference between last year's cost and this year's. Fees are again raised and the spiral continues."

Thus for various reasons we have the private colleges and universities helplessly pricing themselves out of the market, their dormitories emptying. At the same time when the state schools grapple with enrollments swelling at a rate that averages 5.5 percent per year—demand being met with tax-financed public colleges that charge little or no tuition. These institutions in turn add to the problems of the independent school, in particular certain larger urban institutions where only the light push of a finger is needed to tumble the already buckling walls.

The dilemma analogous to the very real condition of walking north on a southbound train is exemplified by my own school, Saint Louis University. During ten years through 1970, our revenues climbed from $14.9 million to $44.4 million. In the same period, however, total operating expenditures grew from $14.9 million to $46.7 million, putting us in the red more than two million dollars.

The increase in the cost of support functions—general administration, operation and maintenance and auxiliary enterprises—reflects primarily the impact of inflation on salaries and materials, supplies and services required to keep the university functioning.

However, these higher operating costs are also the result of our continuing efforts to improve the quality of the education we provide, as measured by such factors as higher faculty pay and departmental research of greater scope and sophistication.

The effect of these efforts has been to increase the university's cost of instruction per undergraduate student from $712 in 1961 to $1,884 in 1970, a 164 percent increase. In the same period, the *total* cost to the university per undergraduate student rose from $1,685 to $4,200, an increase of 150 percent.

It is significant to note that the basic tuition of $800 for a full-time Saint Louis University undergraduate in 1961 covered 47.4 percent of the total cost of his education. By 1970 tuition had doubled, but it covered only 38 percent of the total cost.

During the same period, our average annual student aid increased at the rate of 17.6 percent per year in part because the increases in tuition made it necessary to provide more help to larger numbers of students. But it was also a result of our deliberate effort to provide educational opportunity for more students from lower-income families.

In our case, a major factor in our ability to improve quality and to assume more responsibility for less privileged students was the Ford Challenge Grant of $5 million spread over the three-year period, 1967–1969, years in which we showed comfortable surpluses of income over expenditures. But in 1970, after the Ford Challenge Grant expired, we faced a sudden slide from surplus to deficit. Our effort to close the gap is described on later pages.

Administrations Share the Blame

Some of the blame for today's problems in this private sector, however, must be shared by their administrations. In the process of achieving unprecedented development and some enviable accomplishments during the '60s, higher education like many another burgeoning enterprise reached that point where it became ponderous and increasingly less efficient. Or, the rate and degree of growth accentuated certain weaknesses in administrative practices and business procedures that always had been part and parcel of the system.

No matter—it is neither surprising nor inappropriate that some criticism has been aimed at the front offices of our independent colleges and universities. The charges—and many have been documented—range from inefficiency (inefficient budgeting, inefficient use of facilities, inefficient use of manpower, inefficient purchasing, inefficient programming) all the way to downright fiscal irresponsibility.

During the heyday of the late '60s, realities of budgeting and application of modern business practices were not accorded the sort of attention that went to academic programming, but then they never had been. More and more leaks sprung in the financial dikes as the tide of college and university programs rose and operations expanded. Some of these leaks were very costly.

Preoccupied administrators either did not take the time soon enough to do cost analysis or they did not have the funds. Too few recognized that the number of hours the faculty taught and the number of student credit hours earned under their faculties were dangerously low, even undermining the school's financial health. Too many programs were being launched, some far too costly to be justified. Too few students were enrolled. Nonessential, nonproductive "deadwood" functions, programs and posts at both the academic and administrative levels were tolerated. Characterizing all this was a marked lack of cost consciousness, compounded in some instances by primitive accounting and money management practices. Business-mindedness was not all that highly regarded in the consecrated province of higher education, as some critics have observed.

But it is better to understand than merely to condemn. Mismanagement, where it occurred, was also a matter of colleges wanting to be all things to all students—a seedbed for every kind of greening, as one educator put it. There was a conscientious effort made to be diverse and responsive—honorable intentions which materialized as management misjudgment. The results became ever harder to reverse as enrollments shrunk and outgo began to outstrip income.

It should be mentioned, too, that where certain weaknesses were recognized by an administrator, he could not necessarily correct them. A college or university is dependent upon the agreement of its various constituencies—the trustees, faculty, student body, and various income sources. A consensus concerning policies and programs does not come readily. A college president does not simply call his cabinet together and announce what must be done. Ever-broadening faculty and student participation in decision making has become an aspect of development of higher education during this past decade.

Put another way, a college cannot make adjustments like a corporation if it is to fulfill its mission. Graduating thinkers is different from manufacturing automobiles. No amount of financial genius, accounting wizardry, organizational talent, or gypsy clairvoyance can preclude a deficit when the cost of educating the student rises beyond what the student can pay. If cost accounting can defuse inflation's impact, somebody ought to ask what it really is that is troubling American industry. Granted there are things the patient could have done for itself, but to term the plight of our independent colleges and universities a case of inefficient business practices to be cured with certain adjustments and reforms would be like calling pneumonia an extreme case of runny nose.

Yet it is true that what was on the one hand a glorious hour for private higher education was on the other its hour of surfeit. The greatest surge of growth and development in the history of the private sector also amassed an academic and administrative flabbiness that weakened it for what has turned out to be its fight for survival.

part two

PRIVATE HIGHER
EDUCATION—WHO NEEDS IT?

We have seen that a gross national product of more than a trillion dollars doesn't mean that we as a nation can keep our colleges and universities open, much less prospering. In severest difficulty, as we have noted, are the independent institutions, many of which may be living out their final school year. With bankruptcy imminent, much state and federal legislation now under deliberation seems hopelessly long range. And thus the financial crisis that is cutting like a twister through the groves of private higher education may be allowed to do irretrievable harm —for with the loss of these schools go their traditions and contributions to our way of life.

Could their value to our society somehow have become beside the point?

The real essence of the matter is the question of whether or not the nation really believes that having the private sector and thus a diversified higher education system is worthwhile—not *will* these institutions be around tomorrow, but *should they be?* The gut issue is not inefficiency, waste, or duplication but whether we want the private sector.

Scarcely a Project SEARCH conference missed raising the question, Is the patient really worth saving? "If the private sector claims to be able to offer students something they cannot receive at the public institutions," someone would say, "the parents who will have to pay the bill are justified in asking just what that something is."

It is no easy question to answer. There are no facts and figures to prove that the educational experience of the private college or university is in some way unique or that the merits of such an education have a bearing upon the quality of life later on. The product of the education, after all, is not the graduate at the time he gets the diploma but what he is ten or fifteen years later. Thus it is extremely difficult to evaluate the product of one school or one sector as compared to another.

Today, when the man on the street is frustrated and impatient with the entire college scene in the wake of disturbances and soaring tuitions, his sympathy with schools in distress is scant. He would be hard put to tell you whether a local college is state-supported or independent, and he couldn't care less. When it comes to the private sector, his conception probably is that it is one-third "elitist," one-third so bad it should go under, and most of the remaining third church administered (implying a particular religion's indoctrination—the propaganda arm of the church). To him, the private college or university is exclusive, well-to-do—no place for the kid down the block. Many Americans still harbor the myth that private colleges are wealthy beyond measure and have interest only in students whose parents can perpetuate the condition.

Nothing could be further from the case. Although we do have such institutions, valuable in themselves and often academically excellent, today's private sector is largely made up of colleges and universities that educate children from low and middle as well as high-income families. Many of the students, not to mention the faculty members, are products of "the wrong side of the tracks"—goal-oriented, realistic, committed human beings who work hard for what they get.

There is nothing "elite" about our Saint Louis University student body in terms of economic background. Forty percent qualify for some form of aid. When they enter, we sit them down in the office of our financial aid counselor and see how much they can pay; then we try to get them a job, and then we figure out what sort of government aid they can get. There is usually a gap when it is all over, so we eat the difference. Nothing very elite about any of this.

Are We Losing Diversity?

Also affecting opinion—or the lack of opinion—as to the value of having private as well as public colleges and universities are the increased similarities between the two. Line them up together, say the critics, and you wouldn't be able to tell where one complex ends and the next one begins. Yet in this "age of conformity," isn't lack of individuation typical not just of higher education but of the larger society? How different in character are our factories or their management systems or their products? Our various types of institutions? The agencies of our government? Our life styles in general? Much is uniformity, sameness in the name of economy and efficiency—yet you might argue that higher education should not be faulted for exhibiting the same uniformity, but this would be a specious argument.

If we are to preserve any degree of vitalizing diversity in our society, certainly it must begin in our educational system. To the degree that our colleges and universities have drifted into uniform ruts, they should be sharply criticized. We can only benefit by close scrutiny from our constituencies—including donors, students, parents, and legislators. We must be the object of the freest criticism.

More germane than disappearing differences in form among our colleges are the lessening differences in content of education. As the Newman "Report on Higher Education" observed, "the traditional differences wherein the private school focused on liberal arts while the public one was career-oriented is all but gone, each sector now embracing both types of programs and offering all-purpose education. The uniform acceptance of these curriculum expansions is another similarity. And almost all institutions have the same general image of what they want themselves and their students to be. Both sectors offer similar education programs with like approaches and facilities. Instructors are interchangeable. Thus many traditional distinctions no longer apply except in the small private, undergraduate, liberal arts college which has few public counterparts."

There was a time, too, when the source of financial support differentiated between the sectors, independent schools getting funds from tuition-paying students, and private donors, public schools from taxes. Today we have some public institutions getting more private gift dollars than their independent counterparts, while the latter have turned to state and federal governments for help. Some state universities have larger endowments per student than do private ones.

It is important that loss of distinctive character by schools in the private sector be better understood. There is a distinction to be made between a poverty of individuality on a school's part and uniformity produced by economizing. Where institutions lack adequate funds, they are prey to a kind of economic homogenization process that dissolves the unique, melts down differences, blunts character, and brings a conformity or sameness throughout. For the most part, what is left is an institution with no style or personality, either good or bad.

Diversity and the Church-Related Institutions

Particularly in the case of church-related colleges and universities, character and distinctiveness are in danger of forfeiture in order to qualify for current types of government aid programs. In two separate Project SEARCH conferences (one in Washington and another in New York) Fordham University was brought up as an example of a school having to change its structure because the administration felt that survival was geared to obtaining state help. Said one Congressman, "The result is that Fordham became an institution which is no different today from

New York University in my opinion. I say that quite respectfully, but the point is that its own character is gone."

Charles H. Wilson, Jr., an experienced lawyer with special acquaintance with legal matters pertaining to education has written an excellent commentary on this question. In his interpretation—for the Association of American Colleges, of *Tilton* v. *Richardson*—the Connecticut College case in which his firm* defended the colleges before the U.S. Supreme Court—he recounts that New York's Bundy Law provides institutional grants to colleges and universities based on the number of degrees awarded. But in complying with the state constitution regarding public funds going to church-related institutions, the New York commissioner of education sent a questionnaire to church-related colleges and universities seeking information on the degree of their church relationships. This resulted in twenty-one colleges being declared ineligible!

Obviously schools like Fordham are forced to reconsider certain manifestations of their religious affiliation. Wilson observes that recent Supreme Court rulings have put church-related colleges on notice that their religious functions and activities will be analyzed and evaluated if they hope to participate in education assistance programs. However, no precise guidelines exist to help the institutions determine when they are "too religious." Thus they have tended to become as nonreligious as possible to assure eligibility for badly needed funds. Whether particular church-related colleges have a "substantial religious character" or a "significant religious mission" leads the courts to decide on higher education assistance.

Various criteria for determining whether the religious relationship is sufficiently intense to impose constitutional disability are in use at the moment. Among them: whether the college's governing board includes members of a sponsoring church; whether the school receives financial support from a religious body; whether religious observances are sponsored or encouraged by the college; whether religious affiliation has any bearing on

* Williams, Connolly and Califano.

administrative or faculty posts; the place of religion in the curriculum.

Thus sectarian colleges are lessening their church connections through a variety of techniques—for example, in separating college management from the church and appointing lay members to governing boards.

The Federal Constitution offers more leeway here than do those of most of the states. According to "The Capitol and the Campus" (a report by The Carnegie Commission on Higher Education), "the Constitution of the United States prohibits Congress from making any laws 'respecting an establishment of religion' and through the Fourteenth Amendment this restriction is extended to the states." But the report points to test cases indicating that where a college's stated purpose in relation to religion is not "fervent, intense or passionate in nature" but seems to be "based largely upon a historical background," receiving grants from the state is permissible because the primary purpose is not to aid religion. However, notes the report, "State constitutional problems are not limited to application of the Federal Constitution. Rigid prohibitions against grants of public funds to sectarian schools may be found in thirty-eight state constitutions." Yet most of these states provide some form of aid to their independent schools.

Thus a very real concern in connection with government aid is that it be provided *so as not to ultimately defeat its own goal of preserving a diversified higher education system.* Educators and lawmakers alike are pondering the question of how to provide rescue funds that the institutions so badly need in a manner that accommodates constitutional restrictions on the one hand and does not force diversified education into a homogeneous mass on the other. We will return to this question and take up various approaches and a suggested solution further on.

There are other influences, of course, behind the similarities we see developing among our church-related colleges and universities. Both Catholic and Protestant colleges fifteen or twenty years ago bore the marks of protectionism and propaganda characteristic then. Today this isn't the case.

Taking Saint Louis University as an example of change, in 1967 we converted from an all Jesuit Board of Trustees to one composed at present of twenty-one laymen and women and eleven Jesuits. Thus the body responsible for final policy is more representative of the total community and the various constituencies the university serves.

While retaining distinctiveness, we offer an education without religious requirements that is comparable to any in the nation. In offering to all our students this body of secular education, however, we are maintaining, and in fact, strengthening our identity. Recognizing that universities have had a tendency over the years to remain inherently conservative we have striven to meet the inevitability of change in a way which will allow us to choose and direct our part in that change. When we draw upon the past then, as all universities must, *it will not be primarily so that students may assimilate the present so much as to aid them in creating the future.*

To become more specific concerning the appropriate, if not unique, role of Saint Louis University, it is a Catholic, Jesuit, urban university and each of these characteristics carries with it commitments which must be made complementary with those of the others. The implications of each of these characteristics as they have been hammered out by extensive discussion within the University community are clearly set forth in the "University's Statement of Institutional Philosophy."

The Distinctive Differences

With the preservation of the private sector, we save a *potentiality*. There is the potentiality that the private sector can be different—even very different—and the potentiality that as independent schools, theirs will be a distinctive contribution, whether or not much gets contributed during today's financial depression. This potentiality is part and parcel of independence, and all-important. Once gone, it is gone forever.

The Carnegie Commission for Higher Education has had

this to say on the subject: "It is extremely important to preserve and strengthen private institutions because they innovate imaginative approaches. Also, the greater freedom of private institutions from potential interference helps preserve academic freedom. And the competition of private institutions helps to improve the quality of education in the public institution."

Admittedly, the cash-starved private schools are not living up to such billings at the moment. They are not the innovative factor they once were. But the potentiality is there. Restored to sound fiscal footing, they can again be innovative. Because experimenting with change adds to a school's costs, the public institutions with their larger budgets have been doing much of the educational innovating.

A characteristic of the independent institution such as Saint Louis University that has not diminished, and one that is perhaps more important than any other, is its commitment to clearly define goals. In the public sector, size and numbers as well as dependence upon tax support prevent such commitment. The public institution, almost by definition, must attempt to be all things to all segments of the public. Being committed where a church-related school is concerned is not being propagandistic or performing as teaching arm of the church; a truly committed institution is one that stands for something. The difference lies in this: and I refer to the worthwhile private schools—the independent institution still pays respect to a value system. Such values are very much alive and well on the campuses of many of our independent institutions.

No institution should assume that there are not all kinds of outside influences affecting the student. But the big experience at the college level is maturation of what the young man or young woman believes. Until now, he has been going on gut feeling, or just doing as he has been told. But now, at college, we can fortify those values—give him the opportunity to satisfy his own maturing mind with the reasonableness of these values. We can help him as these values change from gut feelings to rational positions. But put the student into a "factory" environment like that of some mass-production, giant institutions where personal values are either ignored or even laughed at, it will be the rare individual who emerges with clear answers to such ontological questions as "Who am I?," "Where am I going?," and "Why?."

Put another way, the type of private college or university I refer to fulfills a mission that goes beyond transmitting knowledge. It commits itself to producing responsible citizens. Doing what is necessary to achieve this makes our education process a different emotional and a different human experience, though it is difficult to articulate. There is a concern here beyond pumping information into heads as though they were computers. Dealt with is an interpretation of the student's environment, his total existence, him as a total entity. The intention is to fortify him intellectually. We help him develop and defend his standards.

It seems to me that one of our discussants this summer (Fr. Joseph Tetelow, academic vice-president of Loyola University, New Orleans) was right when he observed: "Let's place liberal education, particularly in a private college, solidly on the foundation of the dynamism that is present in a place where young men and women are brought together with older and hopefully wiser men and women for a free and open discussion of values." This is not the traditional concept of a search for truth with truth already wrapped up in packages and ready for insertion into empty, expectant brain cells.

A process encompassing the dynamics of open, serious discussion of values is one that only a college or university can be dedicated to—not the government, church, or other agencies. Because an independent school is free to espouse its own institutional values and commitments, it provides the environment for open, free value discussions. It can be committed to the philosophy that what it can do best is confront its students with the deepest questions of life and make them think about these questions as they apply to themselves.

This learning experience that a private college can provide as a value-oriented institution, it seems to me, may well be the most fruitful argument for the unique purpose and distinctive characteristic of such an institution and for its preservation as a balance for schools that must be tied in with government and a part of massive public systems.

A generation or so ago, many schools, perhaps most, performed an "in loco parentis" function with institutional rules governing personal conduct such as strictly enforced curfews for dormitory residents. Today's more enlightened college or university stands more "in loco amici," supplying guidance and friendly interest in the individual student rather than rigid supervision.

If the objective of liberal education is to become as fully human as possible, the environment of the place of learning should encourage both students and faculty alike to develop deep and abiding friendships. To use the language of the Indian chief in the film "Little Big Man," a private college or university might well make its comprehensive role that of helping young men and women become a "human being instead of a 'white man' "—meaning a human being with all that it connotes of breadth and depth and openness and compassion in contrast to a "white man" with its implications of blindness, provincialism, and prejudice.

The private college deals deliberately with the whole individual and is concerned with what happens to the total human personality during the learning experience at the institution.

A personal slant on the meaning of such an education came during one of the Washington SEARCH conferences. It was offered by Curt Mathews of the St. Louis Post-Dispatch. Said Mathews, "I have attended five private universities in the last fifteen years—Notre Dame, Washington University of St. Louis, St. Louis University, Georgetown University and George Washington University, and there is something about going to a private university that, to me, is an expression of doing your educational thing outside the system. You're not caught up in the industrial–government-oriented or programmed institution. You are doing something apart from this. You are standing off, engaging in an educational experience that is a little bit set aside. There is an expression of individual preference here. It is a matter of individual human dignity, perhaps, if you can step aside and do this thing in your own way. It is something of great value that I hope we will never lose in this country. That a man can step outside the system. Step away from the standardized institution and gain some experience in his own way."

Both Sectors Need Each Other

One of the most important values of our private sector is that it safeguards against a monopolistic higher education system. Its diversity of financial support (individuals, organizations, corporations, and state and local government) provides pluralism of control. Independent, it stands as a countervailing power to protect the public sector and preclude domination of higher education by any interest group or by government. Academic freedom is preserved as students and faculty alike are provided with an alternative to the state system. As a result, our campuses can sustain their tradition of being the testing ground for new ideas, the home for lost causes and a preserve for opposing views. There is room for independent initiative, the prerequisite for change and innovation. As Howard Bowen has stated, "The alternative would be higher education as a monolithic public enterprise." It would be "managed by absentee state boards and central state bureaucracies, heavily influenced by Washington, readily susceptible to politics and often marred by impersonality and uniformity." He adds that "those who have seen at first hand what can happen when a state system of higher education becomes embroiled and entangled in petty politics cringe at the thought of no alternative."

As was pointed out by a college president at one SEARCH conference, "The public or state university must concern itself with what the capitol wants, what it is thinking, and what the interests of the state might be in a given instance. Administrators say to themselves, what does the state budget officer think, what does he really want here? Matters of education become a political hassle. Moreover, the school tends to move in whatever direction it surmises will bring more support from the state for the budget it submits."

In a private institution, in which there is a Board of Trustees who are independent rather than a Board of Regents appointed by the governor, control of programs is sure to remain with the school. Said one private university administrator at another of our conferences, "You'll hear our trustees say that the Department of the Interior or the National Aeronautical and Space Administration is not making the decision with regard to the program in our physics department. Having your department chairman buttressed with that kind of authority is very important to initiative."

By and large, state governmental officials have refrained from interfering in the internal administration of public colleges and universities, so that our historical experience *thus far* tends to minimize the fears we might have about the dangers of a monolithic governance pattern. Still, the presence of the private sector serves a purpose somewhat similar to the "checks and balances" of our political system.

Even though history offers relatively little evidence that government in this country desires to dominate the higher education process, the presence of the private sector assures that such cannot become the case tomorrow. Without such assurance, history in other parts of the world teaches that somewhere, sometime, major intrusions of government into higher education will occur—a particular probability during times of political and social upheaval. It is up to our colleges and universities to continue as sanctuaries for scholars wishing to voice their beliefs and convictions on moral issues such as Vietnam, poverty, and discrimination.

The Taxpayer Needs the Private Sector

Because they fulfill so valuable a role, and because the means do exist in this nation to support a private sector, there are those who maintain that our independent colleges and universities will survive. So too might the Red man have viewed the buffalo. Blind faith alone however will not suffice. And thus the means may remain beyond reach. There are informed authorities who predict that most private institutions will be absorbed into the public system or fold up. Some predict this by the middle 1980s, and who is to argue? The smell of bankruptcy fills the air. Certainly public and governmental indifference at this crucial time would fulfill the prophecy.

The shock wave from such a calamity would be absorbed by the public sector with commensurate impact upon the taxpayers, something not entirely understood by the general public. With three fifths of our colleges and universities being independent, their demise would place an intolerable burden upon the state systems, forcing sizable and unnecessary outlays of tax money for takeovers and expansions. The message that has not yet been driven home to the public is what it would cost taxpayers if faculties and facilities for students now attending independent colleges and universities had to be provided at public institutions.

During our New York SEARCH conference, Allan Cartter, chancellor of New York University, observed that a private institution may be having trouble at the dollar level because its budget is three or four million dollars shy of its operating need. But if the school must go public—has to let itself be absorbed into the state system—the cost to the state taxpayers could be $40 million per year! He went on to say that, like many of our state legislatures, New York's may have to face this dilemma repeatedly during the next few years with Polytechnic Institute of Brooklyn, New York University, and Syracuse among those schools that have problems. If New York University were to go public, it would cost the state some $60 million per year! And if something in the financing structure doesn't change soon, the likelihood isn't that remote. The university is spending unrestricted endowment at the rate of $1 million a month and only has about $20 million left in its unrestricted endowment, according to Cartter.

If the private sector collapsed, the severest stress would be put upon already hard-pressed state budgets to either absorb or supplant these institutions previously funded largely by private sources. The states' outlays for maintenance costs would soar. In some cases, instead of just taking over existing facilities, new state investments would be required to build new or additional ones. Public colleges and universities already bulging would be strained further by the added enrollments. Accommodating these new students would consume funds badly needed for maintaining the quality of existing educational programs.

Reduced to simplest terms, either the private sector is rescued with fewer dollars or the public sector will have to take the whole load, which means many times the rescue dollars that would be required. Assume a state has reported some 20,000 vacancies in its independent colleges and universities: suppose the choice is between (a) tuition grants or some sort of state aid to make it possible for students to use this space or (b) the state's adding a 20,000-capacity to its educational facilities—the difference involved would run into millions of state tax dollars. Clearly then, a forceful economic argument must be included in the answer to our question: Private higher education—who needs it?

An inclusive statement in behalf of the private sector appeared in a recent report entitled "Legal and Political Issues of State Aid for Private Higher Education" by William McFarlane and Charles Wheeler (published by the Southern Regional Education Board) follows:

> As some institutions have grown, they've become less and less 'communities of scholars' and more and more the educational counterparts of large corporate organizations . . . with emphasis on 'efficient production' meaning credit hours, degrees, publications, research discoveries and so forth. . . . All of which tend to divert attention from the essential personal aspects of education, basic qualitative values.
>
> Concern for these values has to come when you consider sheer size with corresponding tendencies to monolithic structures. Other values which can be substantially diminished, if not altogether obliterated, by the emergence of an effective public monopoly in higher education include diversity in educational philosophies and styles and academic freedom in several dimensions. Also, the private sector on the whole reflects a greater measure of individualistic approach to higher education than does its public counterpart.

Be that as it may, no one denies the excellence of many large public institutions and nothing given herein as a value of independent colleges and universities is intended at the expense of the public sector. Rather, the case to be made is for the preservation of our pluralistic system with balanced growth for both public and private colleges and universities. Each sector will be the better for the presence of the other, and thus better able to serve the interests of our young and of our nation.

The immediate task, then, is to restore the pluralistic system's fiscal health. "Higher education has come into hard times serious enough to be termed a depression," we have been told by Cheit in *The New Depression in Higher Education.* "Recovery will not be the by-product of other events like the end of the war in Vietnam or a stock market advance. Rather, it requires deliberate effort to restore school finance."

The patient is worth the effort.

part three

COLLEGE FINANCE— HOW MUCH, FOR WHAT, FROM WHOM?

Long overdue reforms are taking place in both private and public higher education at this writing. And since the independent schools are being hit hardest, their response is the more extensive. Thus in some respects the so-called "depression" that has come to the campus might look to some observers like an opportunity to be met rather than a burden to be borne. However what is being done could amount to a very successful operation resulting in the loss of the patient. Reforms notwithstanding, the patient requires a transfusion of funds. Immediate financial aid is essential, or as one university president phrased it, "Within the next year, the sound of crashing colleges is going to be deafening." An education-oriented management consultant firm recently predicted that "as many as five hundred private colleges will go bankrupt, merge, become community colleges or be absorbed into tax-supported systems during the '70s."

One reason that we as a nation are having to struggle so with the question of what the form and extent of financial aid should be is that we have not clearly fixed the place of higher education among our national priorities. Time and again during SEARCH meetings, participants such as Senator Stuart Symington underscored the necessity for a realignment of the objectives to which we can commit our limited national resources—with education taking second rank.

The crucial need for such a reordering of priorities has been eloquently spoken to by many of our leaders. The Task Force Recommendations of the 1971 White House Conference on Youth call for increasing the national spending on primary, secondary, and higher education from the current level of 3.6 percent of the national budget to a total of 25 percent. Whatever the appropriate percentage might be, it is abundantly clear that millions of dollars should be shifted from defense and probably from even more popular causes, to the categories in the Federal budget that will give America some hope of developing and enriching the mind and the spirit of her citizens—evidence that we really believe it is not by bread alone that man lives. Said Senator Symington, "Nations no longer can shoot their way out of embroilments; they must think their way out."

The solution to the campus monetary crisis is one that depends not on spending more tax dollars but on a transfer of spending—a rebalancing of government outlays—from other less critical areas in time to stop college doors from closing. Such reallocations must take place at both the state and Federal levels, with state and Federal governments acting in concert.

We know that present realities in the private economy do not bode well for financially troubled colleges and universities. However various courses of action are under consideration—Federal proposals, state programs, and measures to be taken by the schools themselves. In subsequent sections, we will evaluate these, but first, let us consider aid broadly, and aspects in it generally arising in any serious examination of higher education finance, especially that of the private sector.

Aid should have these basic objectives: (1) to sustain and improve the quality of deserving schools; (2) to achieve greater equality of access—a choice of institutions by anyone wanting an education. Earlier, when touching on the character of financial support essential to the private sector, the accent was put on diversity—not just business or industry support or donations from individuals and foundations or government funding but support from all of these sources together with tuition. In this way, the institution preserves its independence. It is worth noting that the amount of aid from the Federal government now being considered in Congress would comprise *less than fifteen percent* of the operating costs of private higher education. Help of this order of magnitude will not jeopardize the autonomy of the college.

Philosophies of Financing

There are differing philosophies or views on how the individual's higher education should be paid for. For example, advocates of low-cost public education have impressed upon the public mind for years the notion that because we are educating primarily for society and secondarily for the individual, the American ideal is a costless education. Others have replied that although society should bear a part of the cost (because there are obvious social benefits and because it will encourage individuals to consume more), adult educational experiences are largely undervalued and/or wasted when one does not have to make some personal sacrifice. Therefore the student and/or his parents should contribute.

Allan Cartter said during a SEARCH meeting that his concept of the ideal system would divide the cost into fourths. One-fourth would be covered by Federal grants to students or institutions, one-fourth would be in the form of subsidies from state and local governments together with private gifts and endowments, one-fourth would be paid by parents, the amount adjusted according to ability to pay, and the remaining fourth would be paid by the students, either by way of current self-help or through long-term loans. An intriguing concept—but not one we could implement very quickly. Cartter also said he believed that, were all current direct and indirect education subsidies lumped together and reallocated or redistributed, enough funds would exist to handle our total higher education and student financial needs. Probably so.

Another theory of finance, the simplest of all where state aid is concerned, is exemplified by Governor Gilligan's Ohio Plan whereby public institutions would move toward charging full cost and apply some of the funds previously allocated to subsidize the state system to a massive student grant program. This plan was proposed during the 1970–71 school year but has failed to become the law in Ohio.

The main argument of those who propose this and similar plans is that the student benefits from, and uses, the educational facilities of the state and should, therefore, pay for such facilities.

The arguments of those opposed are many, and to me, convincing.

Basically, the plan provides that students attending Ohio's four year public institutions of higher education agree to pay back the per student appropriations over an extended period of time, commencing when the former student begins earning $7500 (raised from $7000 in the original proposal).

In 1970–71 the State of Ohio subsidized undergradute students at the four year public institutions at the rate of $3000 for four years. This amount represents the state funds paid to the institutions over and above tuition charges.

Students attending public two year institutions would not, under the plan, be required to repay the amount the state expends on their education. If students at such public two year institutions transfer to a private four year Ohio college or university, upon completion of their two year college requirements, the private institution receives the state subsidy which ordinarily goes to a public college or university and charges these students the tuition charged at a public institution.

The amount of the state subsidy paid institutions for graduate and professional students is, of course, higher than for undergraduates. These students would be included in the plan but no student's indebtedness could exceed $15,000.

The shrillest cries of protest rest on at least partially philosophical foundation. The plan is seen as a move away from the American tradition of public responsibility for public education. This is the basis for low cost tuition at state institutions. To abandon such a policy in an age when a college education is viewed as at least as important and necessary as a high school diploma was fifty years ago, would be a mistake. After all, one might suggest that we extend a student's financial responsibility for his own education back to the secondary level and even to the elementary years.

This proposal carries with it a number of possible problems:

1. Students would be encouraged to attend junior colleges, transferring to a four year private college or university, thus, creating a "farm system" although the state subsidy would not be large enough to cover the private school's expenses, especially since the private school would be charging state level tuition.

2. Such an arrangement would negatively effect private giving to both public and private institutions.

3. Reduction in total amount of repayment based on a lump sum payment obviously favors the affluent.

4. There would be difficulty in keeping track of students who move from Ohio as well as the possibilities of a high default rate.

5. Finally, the state, which has been least active and least responsible in assuming its duties toward all of higher education, would be asking the federal government to help students and institutions while refusing to accept its own responsibilities.

It should be kept in mind that under this plan tuition to state institutions is not abolished, and in the ordinary case would still be the responsibility of its students and/or parents.

Any peripheral benefit to low income students by using monies formerly ear-marked for institutions, would be not only questionable finance but would be far outweighed by the faults contained in the plan.

Inasmuch as Governor Gilligan's proposal represents philosophically, at least, much the same situation as a loan, it provides a natural transition into that area of financing higher education.

Are Loan Programs the Answer?

Borrowing as a source of financing higher education has been overplayed by its proponents. Few would argue that the recipient, himself, is not the chief beneficiary of his college education. He is. Nor does anyone deny that investment in a college education is sound, but the weakness with borrowing as a solution is that typically, the student who needs to borrow the largest amount is the one who should be borrowing the least.

Yale University and Duke University have already embarked on their own deferred tuition plans. As pointed out in the October 18, 1971 issue of *The Chronicle of Higher Education*, 22 percent of the Yale undergraduates are participating. The Yale system enables the student to defer up to $800 of the $4400 yearly fees. Saint Louis University's situation is, of course, very different from those of Yale and Duke. We had hoped to be one of several selected universities to participate in a pilot project of PAYE (Pay As You Earn). This proposal had originated with Yale. The Ford Foundation, however, in undertaking to push the plan found that adequate funding from private lending sources was not available. The plan had envisioned the Ford Foundation's providing a substantial amount of money to guarantee loans to be matched by a smaller amount from the participating colleges and universities with the bulk of the money to have come in the form of long-term loans from banks, insurance companies, and other private lending agencies.

Now the Ford Foundation hopes to do research into questions of the legal, administrative, and financial aspects of long-term loans and hopes to work with the Federal government to establish such a program in the future.

Federal Aid: To Student or Institution?

On the Federal level, the most preferred form of aid among educators is the operational grant made directly to the institution. Such funds become immediately available for the school to use where they are needed most. Kinds of assistance, in their descending order of preference among college presidents (according to a Jellema survey reported in *The Red and The Black*) are these:

—Institution grants directly to institutions
—Grants directly to students
—Facilities loans
—A federally supported student loan bank
—Other loans directly to students
—Income-tax credits for student expenditures
—Interest subsidies
—Categorical grants to institutions for research and programs
—Grants to the states for distribution to institutions
—Grants to the states for distribution to students

Although the types of Federal aid may seem numerous, deliberations have come down to what is essentially this choice: (1) continuing to move in the direction of increased student assistance, loans, work-study grants and possibly out-and-out grants through a scholarship system; or (2) pursuance of direct assistance to the institutions based on one kind of formula or another. The pluses and minuses to both approaches have brought a general consensus that we need a compromise plan including the best aspects of each.

Aid to the student, a major part of every current proposal, is just one leg of a three-legged stool. Also needed are funds for the maintenance of the facility and funds for operational expenses—salaries and administration. The latter two legs can be supported more immediately via *unrestricted* institution grants. These have never before been tried. Current categorical grants are restrictive in application and can be used only for specified programs. To the thinking of many educators, unrestricted grants represent the one hope for a timely rescue—the short-term aid needed. In subsequent sections, we will examine and compare these proposed forms of Federal assistance as well as types of state aid. However, some sort of across-the-board institutional aid is needed in addition to any student loans or grants because the latter cover only a part of the operating costs of the school that accepts the student. Granted it is politically difficult to give unrestricted grants to institutions; the trend and the general mentality bend towards specifics—specific aid for specific needs. Yet dealing with the crisis demands that we be realistic whether or not it is politically popular, or else we fail.

Problems Raised by Scholarship Aid

As mentioned in Part I, the hard reality is that current operating deficits of many institutions, including my own, are roughly equivalent to the amount of aid the schools eventually provide to students who cannot pay their way. Low-income students now coming to college with government aid tend to require considerable additional expenditures, some very difficult to pin down. In addition to needing greater remedial class work, tutoring, and counseling, they sometimes also require room and board. But aid to deserving students goes beyond the low-income group to middle-income youngsters as well.

To cite a typical case: a student applies early, wanting badly to attend Saint Louis University. The combination of what he and his family can afford, plus loans, plus a part-time job, totals $1,200. He needs another $700 to meet our tuition. Our choice is to accept him and grant him a tuition remission (scholarship) of $700 or see him go to a public institution.

But it is not really a choice. You can stay alive longer by at least accepting such students who bring with them $1,200. If you do not accept this student, in this day of decreasing enrollment, the university has another empty place and $1,200 less. So the university often opts for granting a tuition remission of $700. Thus, the university's tuition income is reduced by $700.

and perhaps cannot offset its rising costs in this manner . . . no major ways are likely to be found in the short run which will make it possible to educate more students at the same level of expenditures without lowering academic quality."

Academic goals and profit motives require separate criteria for judging administrative performance and goal achievement. A college is in difficulty if its current financial straits have it operating at a quality level below its capability or below the level required to fulfill its educational and social objectives, even though its books balance. There is no necessary connection between academic or educational success and financial success; obviously a degree of the latter is imperative for sustaining existence. Where, as Howard Bowen has said, "an institution's deficit is a gap between an accustomed standard of living and income, and not a gap between the sum needed for good education and income," then the burden must be on the school to adjust. But a school whose "living standard" is already bargain basement can be in financial trouble precisely because it is doing a fine job.

Too frequently, an administrator faces the either/or choice of breaking even or reducing program quality. Reduction of services and programs can spell deterioration of the institution, because quantitative reduction isn't necessarily balanced by qualitative improvement. Thus presidents of our crisis-caught institutions have not merely trimmed back activities to match lessening income. As Earl Cheit stated in his book, "It is important to distinguish methods from goals. Financial condition is itself the goal of a business organization, but it is only the enabling condition of an academic organization."

What Price Efficiency?

While we emphatically do not want to apply less than the best business practices to college administration, such practices must accommodate the learning atmosphere. We may produce graduates faster or more efficiently but we also may produce them less well. A college is more than a production line. More is at stake here than Kleenex or sneakers—though to hear some of our critics, it would seem that the nature of the educational process is nowhere as important as "efficient" production. However, they would not want their youngsters to attend an institution where this was true.

We must ask ourselves how efficient we want a college or university to become. Certainly education should not be administered by the numbers. Educators, by their nature, seek the most fulfilling line between two points, not necessarily the shortest, and colleges must provide the time to work and think.

On that score, Howard Bowen and Gordon Douglass in "Efficiency in Liberal Education" have this to say: "We believe that good liberal education involves more than the transmission of fact and ideas of a kind that can be measured by test scores. It also involves outlooks, attitudes, values, motives and development of character and personality. Therefore it must include significant human and personal relationships between students and faculty and among students. We do not accept the concept that liberal education can be defined as an accumulation of credit or can be conveyed wholly by mechanical or assembly line techniques. Nevertheless, we believe efficiency can be improved."

It should be understood that college administrators do not downplay fiscal responsibility or efficiency but feel that the criteria should be different for evaluating performance and establishing what is efficient on a campus versus a manufacturing plant.

Going further, the Carnegie Commission's, *The Capitol and the Campus* states, "The very things for which we most highly value private institutions—diversity, individual attention, quality, and innovation—are likely to result in higher per student costs." Such are the aspects that reflect themselves not alone in comparisons between public and private institutions but in comparisons by experts outside education with standards of noneducational endeavors. Nowhere is it written that if a university can get by more cheaply and survive, it is serving society better to do so or that higher expenditures must be inefficiencies or "fat to be trimmed from the budget."

John W. Gardner tells us in his book, *Self-Renewal,* that "there is a mistaken conception of efficiency that sees pluralistic approaches as wasteful and confusing. The need for efficiency is not to be laughed off, of course. In a grim world, free societies must prove their capacity to function efficiently. Extremes of pluralism can lead to utter confusion. But creative organizations of societies are rarely tidy. Some tolerance for inconsistencies, for profusion of purposes and strategies and for conflict is the price of freedom and vitality." He might well have been referring to higher education.

Cost Accounting No Panacea

Often, too, unfair comparisons are made between the academic organization and a business with the suggestion that colleges would not be in such trouble if they understood and applied cost accounting. Yet some schools that have practiced it are hurting along with the others. For example, Dr. Willis Tate, president of Southern Methodist University, told us during our first Project SEARCH meeting that his university brought in a business management consultant firm to propose improved budgetary administration and operating practices that would lead the school back to the break-even point. When the firm completed its study, it reported that SMU was doing a miraculous job of getting by on a shoe string.

The fact is that *by itself, even 100 percent productivity or efficiency on the part of today's tempest-tossed independent colleges and universities will not get them by.* Maximum "yield" is not necessarily an antidote for our campus financial ills. More is demanded than cost accounting, revamped business practices, cutbacks, and belt tightening. By themselves, as Howard Bowen said, such measures may only result in death by starvation.

In other words we must keep in mind when grappling with the fiscal quandary of higher education that there are substantive differences between a college and a business. Drive a corporation to the wall and it may make adjustments in its operations that enable it to bounce back; drive a college to the wall and you can kill it.

part four

RESCUE BEGINS AT HOME— THE CAMPUS IMPERATIVES

The most critical problems facing colleges today: lack of funds, unclear objectives, confused and hostile constituencies including students, faculty, alumni, parents and community groups; anachronistic curricula; outmoded and inefficient teaching techniques; lack of enough top-quality teachers and administrators; disagreement about the top priorities; inefficient use of plant and facilities.

> Dr. Clark Kerr
> Chairman, Carnegie Commission
> on Higher Education

While these are the worst of times for private and public higher education, they could be the best of times for reforms, renewal, and rededication. Necessity is the mother of invention where our schools are concerned, too, and the changes being made are significant rays of light coming at our darkest hour.

First and foremost, our colleges and universities have had to become receptive to change and better ways of fulfilling their task. Evidence indicates that by and large they have. There is no place for blind loyalism to the status quo. Also put to rest must be the traditional institutional protectiveness or tendency toward self-perpetuation. In its stead we must have open examination and honest evaluation of the job being done.

Speaking for the private sector, significant changes are on the way—changes in structures, programs, teaching methods, and administrative operations. As Allan Cartter notes, "A new spirit of experimentation and innovation prevails." At the same time, where expansionism is concerned, there reigns a new stern menage in place of once benign if not ebullient support for broadening departments, programs, services, and responsibilities in every direction.

But reform takes more than a dial turn or a presidential edict. As we noted earlier, unlike the corporation, the university moves by consensus, and on few campuses do the administration, faculty, trustees, and students have a prevailing opinion as to what must and must not be done. Yet headway is being made. Agreement is coming more readily with the realization that the private sector is at Armageddon.

Now, if ever, we must show a turned-off public that we are willing to define goals and to deliver accordingly. Now is the time for asking the right questions and for deciding what our relationship should be to the rest of society. Too many schools have lost sight of their mission.

Stamp Out Unnecessary Duplication

We in the private sector have no business simply duplicating what the state university can do; we cannot just offer more of the same or we lose our justification and thus our support. We must strive to fill additional needs—do what they aren't doing or what we're really convinced we can do better. Similarly, public institutions should not arbitrarily duplicate programs already offered by private colleges lest public funds go to setting up a competitive situation that is wasteful of the taxpayer's money. Schools must search out ways to cooperate, plan regionally. Longterm savings may be realized by institutions in a reasonable geographic proximity by even collaborating on programs and sharing resources.

In today's changing society, we must rethink why we are

here and what we can contribute that is unique. We must re-
capture the respect of the public, and that calls for demonstrating
that we have direction, that our contribution is of high value,
and that we are responsible. Our mission is not to keep the
school moving no matter where, as the bus driver who phoned
that he was lost but making record time. Without a destination,
what does it matter how fast we travel?

The private sector has to be sure, in other words, that its
faculties and administrators are truly producing an education
experience that is distinctive and worthwhile. We must not allow
ourselves to be forced into a mold. We must take stock and repel
the creeping rigidity of form and insipidity of content that, as
the Newman Report states, reflect less and less the interests of
society. Rather, we must be responsive to differing needs with
different styles of learning.

Education for Tomorrow

Beyond this, we must turn attention to the future, ask ourselves what kind of world will we have in 1980, 1990, 2000. How
can we prepare our students to take roles then as responsible citizens? We must shape programs to meet these future needs.

At Saint Louis University we have launched what we term
"Project 21" in response to the question, how best can we prepare our students for whatever kind of world we will have in
the 21st century? The undertaking is a redesign of programs together with new approaches to studies, including off-campus
projects and internships that will stimulate and challenge the
students more than ever before—an exciting and relevant bill
of fare prepared especially for young intellectual appetites of the
seventies and containing programs that recognize that university
and student must be constructive participants in tomorrow's society.

Also, our "Project 21" redesign of the university's offerings
and structure has inspired the initiation of a program by which

any student who meets certain qualifications may earn his bachelor's degree in three years without summer courses. We have not reduced the number of credit hours required nor have we compromised the quality of education that a three-year degree candidate would receive. Rather, we will make full use of established testing programs plus supplementary tests of our own to allow students to earn credit for as much as twenty-five percent of their course work.

The economic advantages of such a program to students and their families are considerable. By cutting a year from the time required for a degree, they will save one-fourth of the total cost of an undergraduate degree. Also, students will be able to move on to graduate or professional schools a year earlier, or to enter the job market sooner should they so wish. Or they may "stop out" for a year and still finish at the same time. Their options are increased.

The Balanced Budget—A Must

As for the financial side of getting our house in order, the mood of the public is such that unless we can show that we in the private sector are willing to make sacrifices to reach a balanced budget, we are not going to get support. This means that the immediate goal of every private college and university currently operating with a deficit must be to return to a balanced budget within the shortest reasonable time (two or three years) and with the minimum loss, if any, of academic quality.

Measures for achieving this are being studied and suggested by a variety of higher education organizations, including the new Higher Education Management Division of the Academy for Educational Development and the Subcommittee on the Management and Financing of Colleges, which has been authorized to prepare a policy statement by the Committee for Economic Development.

The harassed administrator must not rationalize away exhortations to balance the budget as coming from specatators, doctrinaire kibitzers remote from where the action is. As a university president who has gone down into the valley of fiscal death and returned alive (at least for the time being), I assure you that solvency is possible and that the cost of its attainment is not unbearable.

Because of the very real possibility of bankruptcy at Saint Louis University, the need was for a short-range plan, one that was practical and brutally realistic with a single purpose: to balance the budget with a minimum academic loss. This would gain time. Without it, time would run out and we would have only the option of planning how best to phase out the university (at least as a private institution) or how to save individual pieces of it that could operate independently. Obviously, the goal was one thing to declare and another to achieve. But the alternatives at a time like this are worse than the difficulties.

No small amount of courage was required by the university to follow a plan that required that we discontinue two schools and curtail or eliminate certain graduate programs. We elected to phase out our school of dentistry, for this was largely a part-time teaching operation when what was needed was a full-time dental faculty. Also, the research and professional-type study going on in this department was conducted in one of the oldest buildings on campus. We would have needed $8.5 million for physical facilities, and $200,000–$300,000 in operating outlays to obtain the necessary full-time faculty.

We also chose to phase out our school of engineering, which had a situation similar to dentistry. The engineering school was relatively undeveloped. It lacked strong research, and developed graduate programs. And we had reached the juncture of either developing it further or closing it.

Also, we brought in management consultants to look carefully at how we were operating and to do a cost analysis. Subsequently, we launched a study of hours taught, number of courses offered per department and the teacher-student ratios. Concomitantly we insisted upon a more careful adherence to the long-established policy defining the teaching responsibilities of the faculty and enlarged the minimum class size for courses at the undergraduate and graduate levels.

Without violating policies approved by the American Association of University Professors, we reduced somewhat the number of full-time and especially the part-time faculty members. In addition, we tightened up the organization and functioning of the nonacademic personnel. Also, we adopted a partial fire and casualty self-insurance program.

The cumulative result will be a balanced budget for 1972–1973 after several years of serious deficit financing (as high as $2.3 million annually). Though the projected '72–'73 budget will be considerably below what we need and want for maintaining and strengthening academic quality, the "purifying" process has placed us in a position to make more effective use of the new economic aid which I am confident private institutions will be receiving in the near future (more on this in the subsequent sections).

During all of this belt-tightening, we learned the importance of keeping the faculty informed. They must be shown the realistic elements of the situation, confronted with the hard facts, and made aware that their jobs are at stake. It is important for them to see that decisions are reached through proper process, with correct reasons, and that cutbacks are sound, necessary sacrifices and not just trimming done across the board.

A hard choice to be made is whether or not to tell the faculty—and the public—the actual severity of the situation. Full disclosure exacts a price in loss of morale that can translate into loss of personnel, student prospects, and contributors—this when high morale, confidence, a good staff, more students, and strong financial support are the very things needed for weathering the crisis. Thus the dire prospect, when aired, may become a self-fulfilling prophecy, with your sinking ship image sinking you.

Yet this risk is tempered in that the institution that lays it on the line likewise shows that it has had the dogged courage to face its problem and to persevere no matter how drastic the cure. Such determination is the most persuasive argument the college can have when seeking financial help.

Needed: Help from Traditional Sources

Financial support itself needs to be of the broadest composition. The independent school must cultivate successfully and continuously an ever-widening base of aid. Nothing that has been said or will be said on subsequent pages about the need for state and Federal support for the private college diminishes one whit the need for expanding the more traditional sources of financial assistance to the maximum. I would evaluate these sources in view of our current and future economy as follows:

1. Tuition must be expected to continue to cover a substantial portion of the total cost of a student's education.
2. Some portion of the operating expenditures of the independent college must continue to be carried by those individuals who are the direct beneficiaries of the institution—the alumni. I see no future for most private colleges if we cannot inspire a substantial number of our graduates with enough loyalty and appreciation to make a continuing contribution to their alma mater.
3. Likewise, those individuals and groups in society, the quality of whose lives depend heavily, albeit indirectly, on private colleges and universities in their area must help. We must work to educate them away from the all-too-prevalent notion that governmental assistance in various forms either has made or will make their contributions unnecessary or unimportant.
4. The need for corporate support is greater now than ever before and it is one that business management is the first to acknowledge. It is a responsibility to be shouldered even in the face of the new tax law, liquidation of some company foundations, stock market vacillations, economic recession, and student disorder.

The ups and downs of our national economy have affected corporate support much less than that provided by alumni or other private donors. Oscar A. Lundin,* executive vice president

---

* Speech delivered at Corporate Leadership Luncheon sponsored by the Council for Financial Aid to Education in Indianapolis in 1971.

of General Motors Corporation, points out: "We and other corporations appear to look upon annual support of education as being something of a 'fixed charge,' a financial responsibility that exists in bad times as well as good."

In a speech calling for even broader corporate aid in the future (it is estimated that by 1980, the total corporate support must begin to approach $800 million annually—more than double the current level), Mr. Lundin had this to say about the campus financial crisis: "If this nation were not committed to offering the widest possible educational opportunity to its citizens, we would have no crisis. We also would have an inferior educational system—and an inferior society."

Continuing, Mr. Lundin said, "Certainly one of the sources of our educational system's greatness is its unique combination of public and private institutions. Never before have people been more free to advance themselves educationally. The diversity of our institutions, with their differing philosophies, acts to preserve freedom of choice, to encourage the independence of mind that acts as a buttress against excessive regimentation, and to stimulate progressively higher quality through competition.

"Much is at stake for our society in the crisis facing higher education," he points out. "Too much, in fact, to allow anything to impede our response. I am thinking, for example, of the climate of tension and unrest introduced in recent years on our campuses by a very small minority of young people—not all of them so young, it is significant to note, and not all of them students. We can be thankful that the vast majority of students recognize such disruption for what it is—a denial of the democratic process and of the academic ideal of open and free debate.

"While campus unrest is much less evident today, it could not have come at a worse time for our colleges and universities —just when they were most in need of society's help in solving their critical problems. Many people did not recognize the unrest as a spillover of similar unrest on our streets and in society in general. They over-reacted. Many accused the colleges of excessive liberalism and permissiveness—policies which they felt encouraged the unrest. College administrators were indiscriminately accused of a lack of backbone in retaliating." Mr. Lundin notes that as a result, there were those supporters who picked up their dollars and went home. Importantly, as the CFAE reports, such action among corporations was rare, with corporate support actually peaking during 1969 when campus disturbance was at its height.

A final point made by Mr. Lundin worth reiterating to our corporate supporters is that higher education today is charged with being "excessively liberal, antibusiness, and that it discourages students from considering business as a career." States Mr. Lundin, "More and more we are learning how baseless such assumptions are. The CFAE, for example, estimates that at least half of all college students today enter business after graduation or after military service . . . . This translates into a minimum of 430,000 new employees every year for American business. Over the past ten years, this invaluable human resource has more than doubled."

Also Needed: More from What We Have

Another urgent imperative for the independent institution centers on making better use of its resources. Every aspect of institutional productivity must be carefully examined for effectiveness. Certainly institutions in the private sector have accumulated their share of "fat." The time for a sensible diet is now.

One of the most thoughtful current treatises on such institutional "dieting" has been authored by Virginia Smith, assistant director of the Carnegie Commission on Higher Education. ("More for Less; Higher Education's New Priority," American Council on Education annual meeting, Washington, D.C., Oct. 7, 1971.)

Wisely she warns against inefficient economies. She notes that delayed expenditures (deferring maintenance, postponing capital projects, delaying program changes) may even be net diseconomies, because the same projects may cost much more later and the need will still be there. But she goes on to caution against resistance to change and cites the attitudes and practices unique to academe that bolster such entrenchment: (1) the notion that highest resource input per student results in highest quality; (2) the attitude that attention to cost is not respectable; (3) the disinterest of many faculty members in the educational process as such; and (4) the tendency to separate academic program development from responsibility for securing revenues for the operating budget.

Dr. Smith observes that the best long-range hope for educational effectiveness lies in scholarly experimentation with the educational process itself.

"Substantial increases in productivity will likely be achieved only through changes in the educational process," she says. Certainly the significant advances in productivity in industry have involved the process of production rather than support functions. In higher education, such changes can occur only with experimentation and innovation in academic programs, in instructional techniques, and in the relationship of the student to the institution." She notes, however, that theoretically, an institution in financial crisis may have the motivaton to undertake the experimentation, but it rarely has the risk capital needed . . ."

Dr. Smith concludes that "those who believe there is a silver lining to the financial troubles of higher education may be sorely disappointed unless the impetus provided by financial stress is combined with the much needed risk capital to permit experimentation with and evaluation of different educational approaches."

Obviously we are coming to understand the process of growth and decline in higher education—how we lose our adaptiveness and why rigidity settles in. We have awakened to the necessity of innovation and the importance of individuality. And thanks to the research, probing, analysis, and criticism that we have been subjected to during the heightening of our financial difficulty, we know now a good deal about belt-tightening measures—immediate as well as long-term responses—and the dangers that accompany them. We know that cutbacks must be thought out carefully if they are not to destroy beneficial developments; that we have no more devastating foe than unguided, witless change. We know that we must avoid a nonselective, across-the-board, panicky reduction of programs, departments, and plans, otherwise our best intentions will be self-canceling, and though our doors may remain open, better they were closed. And we know that short-term self-rescue *is* possible—with a little help from our friends—and that this can buy us the time we need.

Self-Help—The Strategy

The elements of such an attempt are now rather well-identified and can be accomplished without impairing educational quality. They include the following:

1. The school must decide upon its purpose and get back to it. The problem has to be solved philosophically if it is to be solved financially. What is required is a move toward consolidation and enrichment—doing fewer things and doing them well. The institution must think creatively about better ways to do the job. Parenthetically, it was said during our SEARCH discussions that universities sometimes sell their souls to business, industry, and government, which want certain things done that may be inappropriate for schools. It is not the mission of the college or university to train people for industry but to educate, said one administrator, adding that *we need to graduate thinkers, not technicians.*

2. In line with the preceding, a second measure to be taken is to decide what wood is dead where services, courses, programs, activities, operations, and posts are concerned, and then to prune. Administrators must face the reality that programs have to be trimmed and that seeking wider appeal via greater variety of programs can be suicidal. This doesn't mean that core programs should go; those the school does well should remain and be enhanced—here is where appeal should be added.

3. Cost consciousness must become a way of life for faculty as well as administrators.

4. Decrease the level of student services where this can be done and still permit essentials to be met. Costs of everything from

admissions, registration, and counseling, to health service, placement, library services, and other institutional accommodations should be examined for possible economies.

5. Keep student aid expenditures at a reasonable level. This requires careful evaluation of the school's aid objectives and of all aspects of the program.

6. Examine institutional productivity. The number of hours the faculty teaches and the number of student credit hours earned under that faculty directly affect the school's financial picture.

Before continuing to the next measure, let me call attention to two comments regarding faculty workload. Writes Virginia Smith, "Various proposals for economies are based on the assumption that faculty members do not put in enough time on the job. Recent work load studies indicate that the average workweek of a faculty member is sixty hours. Thus forced increases in certain elements of the faculty member's work would generally result only in a decrease of time spent on others." Also pertinent is this comment from the Bowen and Douglass volume, *Efficiency in Liberal Education,* which reads, "It is sometimes said that to raise educational efficiency it is necessary only to raise the teaching loads of professors. On the basis of our special studies of faculty workloads, we believe that a preponderant majority of faculty members are working at full capacity in relation, for example, to the effort of comparable professional people and executives."

7. Make a thorough cost analysis and determine exactly what is being achieved for what is being spent. There are always holes to be plugged. Some may be very big, very costly. One Illinois college recently computed its cost per student per year to be $2,000. But in its astronomy department, the figure turned out to be $9,000 because of the equipment required and the small enrollment in that department. All programs should be examined for the possibility of deletions and combinations of instructors and courses.

8. Strive for still better use of all resources. Every aspect of institutional productivity must be fully exploited. One such effort concerning physical facilities has been the experi-

mentation with a year-round calendar, particularly by the University of California (Berkeley), but with little success so far. Virginia Smith relates that the university still is investigating ways to utilize the summer term effectively as well as possibly returning to year-round operation. But she makes this important point: "Experience shows that long-run savings are not attainable without adequate operating funds in the short-run, and that in a complex system, any single change necessitates further multiple adjustments if the system is to work effectively." This can mean a heavier load on the overstrained budget, leaving the college worse off than originally.

9. Interinstitutional cooperation must be explored in connection with resources and programs so that efforts can be coordinated and complementary, not duplicative or destructive. Where possible, the institution should plan regionally with resources and facilities viewed as common to all. Important economies can be achieved through joint use of expensive equipment—for example, computer centers. In a similar vein, there is the possibility of contracting out particular courses where it is geographically feasible, in order to reduce expenditures. This is already being done with success in instances where it is more economical than developing the course on campus and where a quality program happens to be available at a neighboring school.

10. Better utilize existing resources by seeking opportunities to increase enrollment through types of programs on and off campus that can be implemented without adding faculty or expanding facilities.

11. Determine whether or not the institution is offering too many majors for its financial health.

In sum, the school must examine all its operations to discover possible imbalances of income and outgo, to identify areas of high leverage (salaries, administration, aid costs) where action can bring the greatest relief, and to minimize outlays for services, extracurricular activities, supplies, equipment, and staff travel.

For Church-Related Institutions—
Added Imperatives

Where church-related colleges and universities are concerned, there are added imperatives for renewal. These institutions must demonstrate that they are clearly operating within the rights granted and restraints required by the Constitution of the United States and of the states in which they are situated.

As discussed in the preceding sections, part of the disenchantment and doubt about the distinctiveness of private higher education is applicable in a special way to those church-related colleges and universities which, in the eyes of alumni and others, have moved from a deep religious orientation and tradition to a status of real or apparent secularization.

At no time in our history, it seems to me, has there been a more crying need for church-related institutions which make no apology, either for the secular education they are offering or for the accompanying "plus" which they make available on an optional basis to their students. To operate within both the rights and the restraints of the Constitution, every church-related institution should be in a position to demonstrate two facts: (1) that it is providing secular education as a primary institutional objective; and (2) that its secondary religious objectives do not provide any reason for church-state entanglement or potential political divisiveness.

As to the first fact, a religiously oriented college or university, if accredited and generally recognized in the academic world, has as its primary purpose the same secular education as any other college or university. A degree, for example, from a Catholic college stands for substantially the same amount and level of academic achievement as does a degree from any other college. There are many easy tests of this which can be authenticated without any involvement in the internal life of the institution— for example, determination of admissions standards and academic requirements for graduation, determination of ability to transfer credits to other institutions, acceptability of programs for graduate study, and so forth.

To dramatize the separate purposes of a church-related college consider a senior who graduates with academic honors but who during his senior year, gave up his religious faith. Here the secular purpose succeeded, the religion failed.

Second, the governance and operation of the church-related institution should provide no defensible evidence that governmental financial assistance could cause political entanglement or divisiveness. Catholic colleges and universities, for example, should be separate legal corporations, not owned by any religious or ecclesiastical body, but chartered by the state in which they are located as civil, nonprofit charitable corporations with an educational function. Their boards of trustees must be independent of any ecclesiastical authority, and their executive officers, even though some may be priests or members of a religious order must be responsible in their administrative duties solely to their governing board. Consequently, "governmental entanglement" with a church-related institution would not be an entanglement with any church authority or body but one that would differ in no substantial way from a "governmental entanglement" with Harvard or the University of California.

A related point should be made here to further demonstrate the legitimate separation of a primary educational and a secondary religious purpose: A church-related college must not impose religious tests on its students in admissions procedures, or academic programs. Yet the Supreme Court in the recent Tilton case acknowledged that it is perfectly legitimate for a college to *require* all of its students to attend some courses in theology as essential to the institution's interpretation of a comprehensive undergraduate curriculum, provided that the courses are taught as academic disciplines without the indoctrination or propagation of any particular faith.

The language of the Supreme Court in the Tilton case, it seems to me, supports the position that religiously oriented colleges and universities can and should continue to operate within the rights and restraints of the Constitution. Therefore their future lies *not* in losing their identity, *not* in making less distinctive contribution to the rich variety of educational experiences available to American youth, but precisely in their open commitment to provide a recognized secular education of quality *plus* unique opportunities to become a better man or woman in an academic community that recognizes the supremacy of values and is dedicated to the multidimensional growth of the human being.

For this reason, I am totally out of sympathy with the tendency of some church-related (including Catholic) institutions to go to whatever extreme seems necessary to demonstrate the secular, nonreligious character of the educational experience they offer to their students. Such efforts can only be counterproductive and self-defeating. Once secularity has been achieved, how does the institution justify its existence? Granted many of the distinctive characteristics of a vibrant religiously-oriented institution lie in the area of the intangible and hence defy easy description. But if there are no real differences, it is dishonest to appeal to prospective students and their parents, to alumni, and to donors specifically on the grounds that there are such differences.

Worth keeping in mind particularly in the case of the Catholic institution is that in a day when young priests and religious as well as dedicated laymen are looking for apostolates that are genuine and relevant to society's gravest needs, it is unlikely that they can be recruited for teaching or administrative duties in a college or university which is at best Christian or Catholic in name only.

Accountability—Fair Enough

A final item relevant to the private sector's getting its house in order is that of accountability. This becomes ever more important as we seek government assistance at both the federal and state levels. If we cannot produce usable statistics regarding every phase of our operations, this will be interpreted as either carelessness, mismanagement, or our not knowing what is going on. We must be willing to open our files and reveal our costs— show the number of students we have in our classes, the number of hours our professors are teaching. Only through uniform, accurate facts and figures can the comparisons be made among schools and between the public and private sectors that will enable legislators to get the true picture.

I would argue, though, that public institutions have to be equally open and accountable. To facilitate this, we need to establish common sets of criteria. All of us must follow a uniform practice—not too much to ask of higher education, as I see it, particularly when increased accountability accompanies increased government aid. Under the circumstances, such divulgence of costs and expenditures is neither an imposition nor unfair; any responsible school should accept it and respond to the best of its ability.

To conclude, now is our hour for reform just as it is our hour of need. Granted that most experimentation in the interest of greater productivity, distinctiveness, improvement in the educational process and in operating efficiency requires exactly what is lacking—time and money. The colleges and universities most needing to take the cure are the ones hardest pressed to afford it. We're asking a school that lacks funds and has thinned its faculty to apply risk capital to experimentation and to allocate the manpower to see it through. All of which is not to say that the job can't be done—for it is being done by many schools. My principal point is that such determined self-help needs recognition and all possible support, including—and especially—from the state and Federal governments.

part five

THE STATE'S ROLE—
TO LEAD THE WAY

We have seen that the financing of a balanced public/private system of higher education must be shared by diverse sectors including private individuals and foundations, the federal government, and the states. But the multitude of priorities urgently competing for federal attention place the state in a pivotal position. Its response is crucial, because the state traditionally bears the primary governmental responsibility for higher education within its boundaries. This responsibility has grown, because a college education has evolved from being a privilege for the few to a possibility for all who can profit from it.

There was one hundred percent agreement among our Project SEARCH conference participants that the initiative in higher education belongs at the state level and that the states should continue in their historic central role as determinants of how the postsecondary needs of citizens are met. The alternative to maintaining this responsibility would be to forfeit it to the federal government, making the latter the dominant influence and source of control. If we abandoned the notion that the states should and can assume this basic responsibility and thus abdicate it to the Federal government, we would invite an expansion of bureaucratic problems and have decisions about the state's colleges and universities made a very long way from home.

In "Capitol and the Campus," the Carnegie Commission recommends that "state governments continue to exercise major responsibility . . . for maintaining, improving, and expanding systems of postsecondary education."

When the separate states carry the primary responsibility, responsiveness to local or regional needs is preserved. Moreover, the quality of the educational process benefits by the vitalizing of competition among the states—strong arguments against moving toward a single national system. Federal help should be supplemental in form—supplemental at least at the student level with direct aid going to the institutions themselves. (We will take up proposals for Federal aid in Part Six.)

How Effective Are the States in Fulfilling Their Role?

In 1970–1971 all the fifty states appropriated $7 billion for funding of higher education, nearly $1 billion more than in any previous year. But a great part of this increase went for new facilities and new institutions required by increasing enrollment rather than for upgrading educational quality or support of existing institutions struggling to maintain their regular programs. Most important, some of the expansion dollars were spent in states where *unused accommodations* exist. And herein lies the rub. While taxpayers in those states are sustaining the increasing financial burden of public expansion, independent institutions stand by not just willing, but needing to help.

A number of factors already discussed have contributed to this paradox—most importantly, soaring costs. These costs have risen equally for both public and private colleges, but while the private schools must respond by increasing tuition, the public sector passes most of the rise on to the taxpayer. As we have seen, the resulting higher tuitions in the private institutions force more and more students to crowd into the state schools, with the private college classrooms, labs, and dormitories going empty.

The solution to such a costly and wasteful dilemma is a state-wide comprehensive aid program for independent as well as public colleges and universities. In practice, as some states have already proven, this means that in addition to making optimum use of state tax money and achieving a strong, well-planned, and adequately funded system of public institutions, the state makes it possible for its independent schools to provide their varied programs, adding to the competition, and enriching the state's overall quality of education. Everyone wins.

At the moment, state financial support for higher education varies widely. (These variations are given in detail in the National Council of Independent Colleges and Universities report, "A Survey of State Programs of Aid to Independent Colleges and Universities and Their Students.") The disparity at the state level ranges from no assistance to either students or colleges all the way to comprehensive programs for undergraduate and graduate aid and supplementary assistance to institutions. Currently, fifteen of the states leave the independent colleges and universities out in the cold, though these schools educate a significant portion of the citizenry, including a disproportionate number of their professional people. Taking my own state of Missouri (one of the fifteen), in the five years from 1965 to 1970, *the independent sector awarded 70 percent of the state's medical degrees and almost half the law and dental degrees.*

The Illinois Experience

I doubt that people on the East and West coasts realize the imbalance and inequity that currently characterize state aid. Using Saint Louis University as an example, if I could put the institution on wheels and roll it three miles east to Illinois, I would have an entirely different financial situation. Illinois has one of the most effective programs in the country for obtaining maximum higher education for the dollars it spends; this is achieved primarily through aid to students in private as well as public colleges and universities.

An evaluation of the results of the program was recently conducted jointly by the Illinois State Scholarship Commission and the Illinois Board of Higher Education. It shows that Illinois state scholarships and grants strongly affect college attendance, college choice, distribution of students attending public and nonpublic colleges, and the ability of students to keep loans and part-time work at reasonable levels. The findings prove that the program has diverted large numbers of students from public to nonpublic colleges and has contributed substantially to the economic and enrollment stability of nonpublic colleges in Illinois. The findings also prove that the program has been a resounding bargain for the Illinois taxpayer.

Specifically, the study reports that 5,142 private college students in 1968–1969 would, without Illinois State Scholarship Commission funds, have been enrolled in public colleges. Here is the arithmetic by which the study demonstrates the resulting savings to the Illinois taxpayer: "The estimated cost to the state of operational expenses alone (estimated to be $1,300 per year, per student) to educate the 5,142 students diverted from tax-assisted colleges in 1968–1969 would have been about $6,700,000. Based on these data, the $4,700,000 Illinois has invested in this group in the form of financial aid, which averaged $915 per award, to attend the private college produced a net savings in operational costs alone of about $2,000,000. This figure does not include the additional capital expenditures needed for facilities to accommodate such students. Projected to the 1970–1971 academic year and based on the current average $1,800 per ISSC award, the estimated 9,500 private college students who would otherwise now be in Illinois public colleges represent a net savings in operational costs alone of about $2,850,000."

In the twelve years ending in June 1970, Illinois made 125,000 awards totaling $76,600,000 in the form of scholarships (competitive) and grants (noncompetitive, based solely on financial need). The study shows that the grant program has had a greater effect than the scholarship program on increasing college attendance among students with a wide range of ethnic and racial backgrounds, as one would expect. Students reported that if the scholarship and grant awards had not been available, they would have faced these alternatives: (a) to forego college; (b) to attend a second- or third-choice institution; (c) to work excessive hours, which would have affected the quality of their education; or (d) to borrow large sums of money to meet their educational costs. As the study observes, "The impact of large loans which must be repaid after graduation and after the start of a career and/or family is a subject of concern to many educators."

State aid in Illinois began in 1957 with a state-wide scholarship plan similar to the California plan, that provided talented and needy undergraduates with nonrepayable scholarships to attend *any* approved institution in the state. In 1961, legislative approval came for grants to any student who had been accepted by the school of his choice and who could demonstrate financial need. In 1965 guaranteed loans were made available to both collegiate and vocational students.

In addition to other aid, Illinois has now passed a statute appropriating $6 million for nonpublic colleges and universities. This subsidy for private institutions includes direct grants of $100 paid to the school for each freshman and sophomore state grant or award recipient and a further $200 for each Illinois resident who is enrolled as a junior or senior.

Thus has evolved a state system of higher education that takes full advantage of the assets in being of the private sector to relieve many of the pressures on the public sector. The end result has been beneficial to all the partners in the educational enterprise—the student, the colleges and universities, both public and private, and the taxpayer who foots the bill. The student and his family are much freer to choose the institution that best matches his educational goals. The public colleges and universities are freed from the stresses and strains that inevitably accompany rapid and uncontrollable growth. The richly diversified private sector has been saved from financial disaster. The taxpayer has been assured of efficient use of his tax dollars that support higher education in Illinois.

Thus in Illinois today, any student can apply to the state for assistance, and if the need is there, he can get up to $1,200, depending on what it will cost him at the school of his choice, e.g., Southern Illinois or Northwestern or DePaul. The funding for the 1971–1972 school year has reached $39.4 million and serves some 58,000 students. Missouri residents, by comparison, have no similar assistance from the state. Because the Illinois student receiving aid cannot spend it across the river in Missouri, my own school endures double jeopardy—a dilemma common around the country—wherein there are no state resources available to help us accommodate Missouri residents, nor can we compete any longer in what comprises about half of our primary recruiting region—the Illinois portion of the metropolitan St. Louis area. This has been a major factor in our enrollment decline.

To further amplify what schools like St. Louis University are experiencing, during the 1967–1970 period, over 50 percent of the students who applied to us, and who survived the admissions screening and were accepted failed to show up for registrations.

To Close the Gap

Last year we sent questionnaires to every one of those no-show applicants and to their parents as well. We asked various questions concerning why the students first applied, then, having been accepted, didn't come. We also asked whether they would still come to St. Louis University if more financial help were available. Over 80 percent of the respondents replied that their first choice was and still remained St. Louis University, but that they had settled for another school where their outlay was less.

Other urban colleges and universities suffer similar serious geographic handicaps. Where state lines divide metropolitan areas there is serious need for area-wide planning and cooperation to achieve the most efficient use of the community's resources in higher education. Of course the overriding need is a parity of aid among all states.

In point of fact, with some states meeting their responsibilities of providing comprehensive help and others not, geographic location is becoming a more crucial determinant of a school's economic outlook and a student's chances to achieve the education he desires. For example, a $12,000-income family on "A" Street in St. Louis whose son wishes to attend a specific independent college cannot afford his choice. A $12,000-income family five or six miles away on "B" Street in East St. Louis, whose son also chooses a private institution, receives a grant-in-aid and is able to enroll in the school he feels will best meet his educational goals.

For the East St. Louis student, the state contribution in the form of a student grant, however modest, makes the difference. For the Missouri student, a tuition discount by the private school, plus a part-time job and a federally guaranteed loan often falls short of what he can afford. The gap may only be $300 or $400, but it is usually enough to divert him to one of Missouri's rapidly expanding tax-supported institutions.

The kind of state aid program that helps close that gap has been adopted in about 35 states. Fifteen have yet to take any action. Thus, as in Missouri, the private school loses the student, and the issues not dealt with include (1) the decreasing enrollment of the financially distressed private sector; (2) the overcrowded conditions in the public institutions; and (3) application of tax dollars to achieve greater quantity and quality of postsecondary education for the state as a whole.

The Missouri Experience

Again using my own state as an example of a widespread current situation, during the 1960s total enrollment in accredited public and private institutions increased almost 120 percent. Virtually all this growth was in the public sector. Enrollment in the thirty-four member institutions of the Independent Colleges and Universities of Missouri (ICUM) increased slowly to a peak of 39,095 in 1966–1967, then began to decline as the tuition gap between private and public sectors continued to widen. By 1969–1970, total undergraduate enrollment in ICUM institutions was down to 34,937.

In the fall of 1970, a Governor's Task Force on the Role of Private Higher Education in Missouri reported that close to 9,000 undergraduate vacancies existed in the private sector. Yet that same fall, newspapers reported that the University of Missouri–St. Louis had to turn away 500 qualified students seeking admission. They also reported on an admissions crunch at other tax-supported institutions. At the same time the public schools were being swamped with students, they were being starved for dollars by an increasingly relunctant state legislature.

Under legislation recommended by the Governor's Task Force, it would have been possible to relieve the pressures on the public sector by using the vacancies in the private sector at a per student cost to the taxpayers of less than one-half the average cost for students enrolled at the University of Missouri and State colleges. For many reasons not germane to this section of my report, the legislation failed to pass. We will try again.

Another graphic illustration favoring aid to the private sector rather than eventually having to acquire the load that it bears was provided to Missourians not long ago when the state took over the University of Kansas City (Mo.), a private school, and made it a branch of the University of Missouri. What had formerly been operated as a private university without any expense to the state immediately required an appropriation of close to $4 million. In 1968–1969, the University of Missouri at Kansas City received a state appropriation of $13,700,000.

The Taxpayers Lose

When the taxpayers come to understand the inequity and the lack of economy that characterizes such a development, it will stop happening. That there is a ridiculous waste of resources here is a conclusion people will all reach—but they must reach it soon. So far, the discovery has been far too gradual on the part of citizens in too many of our states. The economic realities dictate (1) supplemental state assistance to fill the budget gap

Many state constitutions prohibit grants of public money to private individuals and also call for separation of church and state, which raises a question where a student receiving a grant might choose to attend a church-related college or university.

Regarding constitutional provisions prohibiting the grant of public funds to a private individual, judges and legislators throughout the country have uniformly concluded that programs in aid of higher education, both public and private, are general welfare measures which serve the public interest. Grants to private individuals under such programs therefore serve a public purpose and confer a significant though intangible benefit to the state. Ten of the states which have adopted programs providing grants to students have constitutions that specifically prohibit the appropriations of public funds for private individuals. Yet in all ten, student grants are interpreted as serving the public interest and therefore exempt from the prohibition.

Whether the use of a state grant by a student to attend a Church-related institution of higher learning violates the church-state prohibition of state constitutions depends primarily on how the enabling legislation is drafted. Most legal authorities agree that no constitutional problems are raised if the legislation (1) has a clearly secular purpose; (2) has a primary effect that neither advances nor inhibits religion; and (3) does not result in an excessive government entanglement with religion. In any one state and with any one piece of legislation, the final authority, of course, is the Supreme Court of that state. However, it seems clear that the church-state issue is in no way a valid objection to an effective program for making full use of a state's higher education resources, both private and public.

"Legal and political issues need not comprise insuperable obstacles to judicious use of state support," states the McFarlane/ Wheeler report regarding the legality of state aid. The position of these experts is that state initiatives to develop private sector subsidies encompass economic and educational goals that are in the public's interest. Such subsidies, they point out, can promote a more efficient use of tax resources allocated to higher education. They also suggest emphasis on ways state subsidies could encourage public and private institutions to cooperate in serving the larger public interest.

What then is the legitimate expectation that citizens may harbor regarding their own state's provision of higher educational opportunity for their children?

A considerable portion of Project SEARCH time and deliberation went to consideration of the advantages and disadvantages of various existing state aid programs, examination of the ramifications of the church-state constitutional problem (sharper at the state than federal level in some aspects), together with an effort to envision at least Step One of a coordinated plan for state and federal efforts in higher education assistance. At least two programs seem absolutely essential for all states, one at the undergraduate and the other at the graduate level.

AT THE UNDERGRADUATE LEVEL.   All things considered, the most viable form of assistance from the state is a tuition equalization program whereby grants based on financial need are awarded to students to help them meet the higher tuition that must be charged by the independent college or university. However, in fairness to the public institutions, these grants should be available to students attending the state schools too. The amount of the individual grant should depend on the financial need of the applicant according to the cost of the education program he has chosen and the amount of funds he can secure from all other sources, including parents, job, Federal aid, and grants-in-aid from the college or university's own funds. The maximum amount of any grant should not exceed the average per student cost to the state for undergraduates in the public institutions.

Without exception, everyone would gain from such a state program, for it would achieve the following:

1. Restoration of freedom of choice to young people and their parents by allowing them to base their choice of institution on types of programs offered rather than on a strictly economic basis. A choice can be made of *any* institution in the state.

2. Permitting the state to concentrate more of its appropriations on providing quality programs rather than meeting the growing quantitative demands for more and larger faculties and facilities.

3. The saving of taxpayers' dollars by making use of existing private vacancies, thereby reducing the need for costly brick and mortar expansion of public institutions and cutting the per student education cost to the state.

4. Assurance that the state, by recognizing the public service of private colleges and universities, will preserve a balanced comprehensive higher education system.

AT THE GRADUATE LEVEL. Necessary to support the tremendous cost for providing graduate and professional training for substantial numbers of a state's doctors, dentists, lawyers, architects, social workers, and other professionals is state assistance covering a portion of the load. Most appropriate is a contractual relationship whereby the state contracts with its private colleges and universities to train its residents. In return, the schools are reimbursed for a portion of the educational costs. One approach is for the state to grant the institution a per student subsidy for each state resident enrolled in a particular program—for example, medicine.

In few areas of our national life is there more deep concern for adequacy than in health education and research and the delivery of health care services. At the same time we are enduring an increasing shortage of medical and paramedical professional personnel. In a number of states, Missouri again being a case in point, the public depends heavily on the output of doctors, dentists, and nurses being educated by the private institutions that are desperately struggling to finance this most expensive type of education.

Similarly, state, community, and private welfare agencies are dependent upon the supply of graduates from private as well as public schools of social work; likewise, the demand continues for graduates in the legal profession. The story is the same with most other fields. Certainly, then, it does not make sense to use tax dollars to plan and build state professional schools when the facilities and professional faculties are on hand within the private sector. Instead of paying the whole cost—astronomical when starting from scratch—the state can readily satisfy its need for the fraction it would reimburse its private schools.

One of the states that contracts with private institutions for educating professional manpower is New York. Schools of medicine are awarded $1,500 a year for each student working toward a medical degree. Awards to institutions training nurses range from $300 a year to community colleges for each New York student enrolled, to $2,500 for each BA degree granted in nursing. In addition, the state encourages the expansion of professional facilities by allowing $6,000 for each additional medical student enrolled and $3,000 for each additional dental student within limits designed to prevent overexpansion of any one school in any one year. The New York program also recognizes the high cost of educating students for advanced degrees by providing $400 for each degree granted at the Masters' level and $2,400 for each doctoral degree.

Somewhat less complicated but at least equally as helpful to institutions training medical doctors and dentists is the legislation adopted by Congress in January 1971 for the District of Columbia—this provides grants of $5,000 for each full-time student enrolled in private nonprofit accredited medical schools in the District of Columbia and $3,000 for each full-time student in private nonprofit accredited dental schools.

From all that has been said, the reader may assume that all states must recognize that they cannot afford to lose educational economic and social assets of the magnitude of their private sector of higher education and thus are in a mood to take the necessary, positive action. This is an unsafe assumption. Those states which refuse to listen to the alarm still exist where politics or public somnolence retard any positive reaction that might increase the chance of survival of their threatened system. There is a necessity here for choice, however, and to ignore it is to choose all the same. By ignoring it, they choose to allow their independent colleges and universities to crumble before the immutables of inflation and apathy.

At the moment, it would appear that while many states are choosing more educational opportunity for fewer dollars through enlightened assistance to their private sector, there are those states willing to accept less (fewer educational opportunities, and a loss of diversity) at a higher level of total costs of educating all students by writing off so vital a resource as their independent colleges and universities.

part six

FEDERAL AID—
IMMEDIACY THE KEY

What should the Federal approach be vis-à-vis aiding higher education in general and the private sector in particular? It was this sort of nitty-gritty question that pervaded much of our Project SEARCH deliberation. That there is a distinct connection between what the Federal government does next and whether tomorrow comes for many colleges and universities, we have noted. Zeroing in on that next move in particularly erudite fashion were participants in our two Washington conferences, men who know enough to write legislation on the subject—the U.S. Senators and Representatives drafting current higher education bills for our land. And in fact, our attention centered on the Federal aid approaches embodied in two of their efforts: the House Bill proposed by Rep. Edith Green (D–Ore.) and the Senate measure sponsored by Sen. Claiborne Pell (D–R.I.).

Exploration of the full range of implications and eventualities wrought by these proposals was the order of the day, though to do them justice might well have taken us the rest of the year. We did, however, deal to some degree with these questions:

1. Should not the present Administration emphasis on assistance to students be at least partially supplemented by programs

deliberately aimed at general support of the institutions themselves—both public and private?

2. How can the Federal government motivate any lagging states
to initiate or improve their assistance to all types of higher
education?

3. Is it wise to place major emphasis in Federal legislation on
borrowing in order to meet either the student's or the institution's costs of higher education?

4. Does the present thrust of Federal legislation toward providing
equal educational opportunities to disadvantaged and minority groups tend to neglect the financial needs of the middle-
income family as well as of the private institutions themselves?

5. Should Federal grant programs for construction of educational
facilities take into greater account the availability of facilities
at neighboring institutions?

6. Should future Federal legislation include more explicitly the
objective of strengthening the pluralistic system of higher
education and therefore provisions deliberately aimed at special assistance for the private sector?

Before going any further, I think it is important to state
that when the private sector beseeches the Federal government
for consideration, it does not do so with any thought of lessening
its own all-out effort to help itself. Nor is there any thought of
substituting Federal aid for the other traditional sources of financial assistance—alumni, private donors, the corporations and
foundations. When we turn to government, we do it only for
supplementary assistance. Earlier I noted our dedication to the
principle of diversified support to preserve autonomy for the
institutions. I think Allan Cartter put it well when he said,
"The Federal government with its national perspective and
revenue base is in the best position to assure that higher education achieves national objectives, but it is the minor partner in
the general support of education." May it ever be thus.

At the same time, we are keenly aware that the Federal government is already doing all sorts of things for higher education
for which we all are grateful. Nor do we imply that we would
change that. Categorical grants have been the backbone of
financial support for research and education for the professions.

Construction grants likewise have been important. The G.I. Bill was a massive benefit, and the subsequent student loan program authorized by The National Defense Act (1958) brought higher education within reach of countless thousands of young Americans. The Higher Education Act (1965) introduced the first Federal scholarships for undergraduates to further extend the opportunity, as did the government-financed work-study grant to institutions, to cover the major share of wages paid to students needing earnings from part-time work to pursue their education. All these measures have been of incalculable benefit to both the independent colleges and universities of the nation and their public counterparts.

Nonetheless, though the Federal role in higher education has been important and is of a more diverse and complex nature than is generally understood, it is still an incomplete and unfulfilled one. To understand how so, and to bring us to what our Project SEARCH recommendations are for fulfillment, it is necessary to consider the Federal role as a trinity taking these forms:

1. The Patronal Role

It is my strong conviction that one of the most vital roles of the Federal government is to give formal endorsement, as the official spokesman of our nation, to certain manifest principles that assert national policy regarding higher education. Though it might be coming quite late, Congress should preface any legislation on higher education *with a clear and indisputable statement of the desirability if not the necessity of a diversified pluralistic system of colleges and universities.*

Some will argue that in itself such a declaration has little practical value, but I do not agree. All Americans, and particularly those of us who are now struggling to keep private higher education alive, need to know whether this nation really wants a continuance of our diversified educational tradition, or whether, for whatever good or poor reasons, it has decided to support only a public system.

Whether assigning those who are dedicated to this principle the role of patron or sponsor or endorser is not too important—what is important is that it be stated loud and clear that this is what we want for our country. An official declaration from the people's representatives at the national level is needed to make very clear that the existence of our independent colleges and universities is held an imperative worth honoring—this will give the general parameters within which private higher education can be expected to live and grow and function in this country.

2. *The Complementary Role*

Perhaps because my experience has been totally with a state that has not distinguished itself in supporting either public or private higher education, I am not optimistic about the states generally assuming their primary responsibility for supporting a comprehensive higher education system. Nevertheless, I believe we must not lose sight of the fundamental premise that the Federal government, particularly at the broad collegiate level, should play a complementary or secondary role to the states. The primary obligation should continue to rest with the latter.

Until more of the states do a better job of fulfilling this obligation and until the disparity of attitudes toward and support of a comprehensive pluralistic system is significantly reduced among the various states, the supplementary role of the Federal government will undoubtedly have to be a substantial one, but this should be a temporary, transitional situation.

3. *The Incentive Role*

The incentive role is directly related to the complementary role just described. In general, the Federal government should not substitute its tax money for programs that states should support. Rather, the Federal government typically should initiate only those programs which it is clear the states cannot finance, but which represent such universal need and interest that Federal support is necessary. Such, for example, in higher education, are the categorical programs sponsored by The National Science Foundation, The Atomic Energy Commission, and The National Aeronautical and Space Agency. But where the states are failing to assume their full obligation, the Federal government should include in its complementary programs incentives intended to urge sluggish states to use their resources more effectively.

A most appropriate application of this incentive role would be in the area of student aid. Assuming that a parity of state aid to higher education is desirable and appropriate for our land and that toward this end each state should have its own tuition equalization program, the Federal government might well introduce into its student aid plans (educational opportunity grants, work-study grants, Federal loans) some measure whereby every state would have an added incentive to either initiate or enlarge its own student aid program.

The educational opportunity grants section of the proposed Senate bill does contain an incentive provision insofar as it authorizes $50 million to be appropriated through fiscal year 1975 for grants to states on an even-matching basis. The measure is to encourage them to provide grants to needy students.

"Project Search" Analysis and Conclusions

Given the broad roles just defined, what sort of general Federal program is needed *immediately* to sufficiently bolster our sector enough to outlast this economic maelstrom?

As has been stated, without some short-range, stop-gap aid, many fine independent colleges and universities won't be around to take advantage of a better tomorrow. To keep distressed schools from reaching that point of no return, our Project SEARCH consensus called for a new and different type of Federal support, one that would supplement what some states are doing for private as well as public institutions, and that would stimulate those states not meeting their obligation to get on the ball. Such a program may not be the ultimate answer nor the best long-term solution, but it will prevent the imminent collapse of a good portion of our independent colleges (including some of our best).

At our Project SEARCH gatherings we attempted to sort and weigh a variety of steps that the Federal government might take in terms of (1) how fast they could be implemented, (2) how likely they would be to win public acceptance, (3) compliance with the Constitution and recent Supreme Court rulings, and (4) practicality—how likely would the program be to get funded if passed by Congress. The approaches have boiled down to whether the Federal government should give an amount of direct support to institutions or only to students, or some combination of the two.

There are many arguments both for and against a number of Federal proposals aimed at accomplishing the general purpose of helping all or most of higher education out of its present fiscal morass. The Senate has already passed legislation known as Senate Bill 659 which is based on the number of disadvantaged students attending an institution. The bill passed by the House, known as House Bill 7248, originally called for grants based on a capitation formula, e.g., number of full-time equivalent students enrolled. At the present time this bill contains stipulations that two-thirds of the money should be distributed on a capitation formula and one-third on a "piggy-back" formula as in the Senate version. When the term "House approach" is employed in connection with legislation, it refers to the capitation formula.

THE SENATE APPROACH.   The Senate bill, sponsored by Senator Pell, calls for direct grants to needy students and a "piggy-back" supplementary allowance (for cost of education) to the college or university for each federally aided student that enrolls.

The key word here is *needy,* for students qualifying would

be those whose meager family resources permit them to make little or no contribution toward paying tuition.

In effect then, this approach attaches institutional aid to the assistance provided the economically disadvantaged. Specifically, each college or university would receive a cost of education supplementary grant determined in amount by the number and level of students at that institution who are receiving Federal assistance in the form of a basic educational opportunity grant.

What we have then is an incentive program wherein the Federal government will supply institutional assistance as a reward for schools according to the opportunity they provide for the needy to achieve higher education.

There are several reasons why I believe that the Senate formula of supplementary grants is much less desirable than across-the-board institutional aid.

1. The main purpose of institutional aid is not simply to provide equal opportunity. Equally important and in one sense prior to equal opportunity is the existence of a diversified, pluralistic system of higher education in the United States. The Secretary of Health, Education, and Welfare, Elliot L. Richardson, in a statement before the Sub-Committee on Education, Committee on Labor and Public Welfare, United States Senate on Wednesday, June 9, 1971, stated that "all of these bills have been introduced largely in response to deepening concern about the financial health of our colleges and universities." There is considerable doubt that Federal support to selected institutions will accomplish this. While totally in sympathy with the motivation behind such a thrust, I am concerned that the very success of enrolling large numbers of low income students is unbelievably expensive. Saint Louis University is a case in point. The results of a study reported in the March 29, 1971 issue of the *Chronicle of Higher Education* illustrates the unusual efforts we have made to enroll Black students, most of whom are economically disadvantaged. The study reveals that our percentage of Black enrollment rose from 1.3 percent in the fall of 1968 to 6.2 percent in the fall of 1970.

The cost of tutoring small classes, specialized personnel and equipment and prolongation of the learning period, may well have been predicted but there are, in addition, hidden costs inevitably involved in overcoming the effects of the cultural and the academic shock experienced by young minority students, who make up a large percentage of the financially disadvantaged, as they endeavor to cope with membership in the university community. They need special help to cope with thought patterns, values and ways of saying and doing things that are totally foreign to anything they had experienced in their own lives. One Ford Foundation official has stated:

> Though our grants to help colleges and universities educate minority students have been many and generous, judged according to enrollment standards, it is now clear that we have helped to lead many of these institutions down the primrose path of fiscal insolvency because of all the unanticipated costs this type of education involves.

2. No matter how generous the forms of Federal student aid may become in the future, and no matter how many students bring with them these kinds of assistance, I am convinced that what really will happen will be that the cost-of-education-supplement will be more than wiped out by the added expenditures generated by the increasing numbers of low income students.

3. If the institution happens to be private, these growing education expenditures, not funded by federal aid programs, will have to come out of institutional funds in the form of tuition remissions, the very factor that is already creating much of the financial trauma in the private sector today. The procedure, therefore, includes a self-defeating, counter-productive force which could be deadly in its consequence.

4. Paradoxically, in order to merit badly needed assistance, an institution is pushed in the direction of a recruitment policy which may be against its best judgment and interests in the light of its total resources.

5. While it is true that heavy reliance must be put on state and private sources, the fact is that for constitutional and other reasons direct state assistance may never become generally available to private institutions. Practically, therefore, the major

role of the state vis-à-vis private education will have to be carried out via the student and the Federal government will have to concern itself for at least some time in the future with some form of more direct assistance.

6. The Senate approach would not really give low income students a chance to attend the institution of their choice if such an institution happened to be private. While those arguing in favor of such an approach point to the availability of loans to meet the expenses of high cost institutions, it is common knowledge that a good many students, especially those whom the Senate approach is intended to assist, will not, and in some instances cannot, obtain an adequate amount through loans.

7. Many of the proponents of the Senate approach are admittedly, at least by implication, more interested in providing some type of education than in giving a student his choice, as exemplified by their recommendation that low income students attend a local, low-cost public institution.

8. Existing and expanded aid to developing institutions would answer, at least in part, the needs of the students the Senate approach seeks to meet.

9. The Senate approach is unfair to middle income families. The main burden of any raise in tuition which would be necessitated by the increase in the number of economically disadvantaged students would fall most heavily on students from middle income families.

10. In many private institutions the student aid costs are the single largest contributor to the institution's financial plight. The low income student is that student, who by definition, needs institutional student aid.

THE HOUSE APPROACH.   The House type of Federal response to the college financial crisis is embodied in a proposal (HR 7248) originally introduced by Representative Green that advocates direct institutional aid keyed to the number of full-time students enrolled. An extra dividend would be paid to small colleges.

The amount of this operating subsidy would increase from freshman through senior to graduate student—recognizing that the cost of educating a college student escalates as he moves up the ladder. More than other approaches, this one could deliver the immediate rescue monies that the independent colleges and universities need. Here, a grant would come with no strings attached and be immediately available for the schools to apply where they most need it. The student grant provision of such a bill could continue along present lines, with the institution's financial aid officer determining the student's eligibility for aid, including scholarships, work-study grants, loans and so on.

It also has been proposed, appropriately, that the family income ceiling be removed, leaving the student aid officer to determine, in terms of all surrounding circumstances, whether a subsidy is essential to the student's being able to attend college—a viewpoint which acknowledges that middle-income students also deserve and may need help.

For the following reasons, I support the general institutional grant approach:

1. The mere fact that such legislation would represent a strong stand on the part of the Federal government in favor of a pluralistic system by assuring direct assistance to each individual college and university as a contributing cell of the total organism of higher education.

The first reason relates to the earlier mentioned patronal or advocate role of the Federal government. There would be far-reaching salutary repercussions from the type of Federal assistance program that manifests this nation's dedication to a pluralistic system. There is no more tangible way to do so than by directly assisting each deserving college and university.

2. Another argument for such comprehensive, unrestricted aid lies in the virtual unanimity of support for it among the diverse segments of the academic community, including the National Association of State Colleges and Universities and the Association of American Colleges. Such solidarity is a phenomenon that argues strongly for the merit of the plan. Wash-

ington long has said that Congress would find it easier to listen and respond if we spoke with one voice—that if we all said the same thing, they'd know what to do. Here, for the first time, we are.

3. In spite of some weaknesses in direct across-the-board aid, no other approach would accomplish the desired objectives as adequately for *all* types of institutions or accomplish them as immediately.

4. Regarding the legitimacy under the Constitution of a direct grant to institutions, this approach does not present any more serious problem than the indirect cost-of-education subsidy included in the Senate-approved measure. While it is true that the indirect plan has the advantage of precedence in the G.I. Bill, nonetheless, without pretending to be a legal expert, it would seem to me that the Supreme Court ruling in the Tilton v. Richardson case allowed ample room for direct assistance within the Constitution's framework. This is the conclusion of Charles H. Wilson in his excellent and comprehensive interpretation of Tilton v. Richardson.

Among other supportive statements, the Supreme Court recognized a fundamental difference between education at the elementary-secondary level and at the higher level. It pointed out that there obviously is a secular education which can be provided by an institution under any auspices; and it emphasized that the matter of governmental involvement or entanglement with religious matters calls for judgment in particular circumstances—it is not something for which hard and fast general rules can be established.

No substantial reason can be seen, therefore, why, with the safeguards already included in House Bill 7248, federal grants could not be made in compliance with the Constitution to any accredited institution, including church-related schools, for operational support of the secular education that it provides.

5. Although some would argue to the contrary, the autonomy of an institution might better be sustained by across-the-board grants than by the categorical grants authorized by the Federal government in past years. Although a new relationship

between the government and private institutions would be initiated, the grants would necessarily be:

(a). Small in relationship to the institution's total budget and the multiple other sources on which it will continue to depend.

(b). Unrestricted as to the use of these funds or at most restricted to the general non-academic operations.

6. This type of grant would allow schools to look for a diverse student population rather than concentrating on increasing disproportionately the number of low income students.

7. The House formula will not, as some seem to think, protect weak colleges and simply perpetuate the status quo.

There are forces for change at work on our campuses today far greater than any posed by Federal aid of the magnitude we are considering herein. To keep the electricity switched on, our private colleges and universities have undertaken exhaustive self-examinations preparatory to major overhaul. To these are being added almost daily demands for innovation and change from every direction—government, private organizations, foundations and from educational associations. Nothing brings out creative instincts, if not the funds to exercise them, like a tight budget, and no one is more anxious to come up with that new approach, that strikingly imaginative innovation, that new look for school and programs than those whose livelihood depends on it—the educators and administrators manning our institutions of higher education. Changes are a must to halt the economic slide of their schools. Changes are a must to remain in competition, for the race is on to come up with the more exciting educational experience. Change is being forced by the changing times, the changing student. No concept goes unevaluated, no aspect of the school or its program is escaping challenge. This is today's higher education environment.

Motivators and/or critics firing from all directions have riddled any vestige of status quo that might somehow have remained after the student disturbances, economic disaster, program cuts, faculty lay-offs and college closings. That any "status quo" could be preserved by forthcoming Federal aid is as likely as Halley's Comet appearing three days running.

With regard to sustaining those institutions that don't deserve continuance—and there are undoubtedly some whose circumstances are such that government assistance would be a matter of putting good money after bad—any Federal grant received would not be enough to save them. Moreover, such an institution will be pressured to capitulate by tomorrow's renewed private sector—necessarily more dynamic, competitive and stimulating than ever before. Competition, remember, is as much the foe of status quo in education as in commerce. It is the early restoration of vitality and competitive spirit to the private sector that the direct institutional grant, together with comprehensive state aid, will achieve.

8. Worth considering too, is the fact that the Federal government would put itself into the accrediting business if it undertook to separate those "unprofitable servants" from the eligibility list for aid. Remember that the approach embodied in the Senate measure does not solve this problem of sustaining the marginal college either. Suffice it to say that all of us are realistic enough not to argue that there is any Federal program in education or any other field which can guarantee 100 percent effective use of every dollar invested in the recipient.

9. The argument that the House approach would encourage the states to reduce their state appropriations for higher education by the amount of the Federal monies received could easily be answered by a section in the enabling legislation providing safeguards against such a contingency.

Currently, the Senate and House versions have not yet been reconciled and the final outcome is, of course, still in doubt. There appears, however, to be a good chance that at least some direct institutional, across-the-board aid will be retained.

Other Areas of Federal Concern

In addition to implementation of a badly needed institutional aid program, other general types of programs at the Federal level need to be strengthened. The following is a synopsis of our Project SEARCH consensus regarding such efforts.

STUDENT GRANTS. The programs in the student aid area, originally and laudably aimed at opening up educational opportunity to the low-income disadvantaged youth of America must be continued, but their purview needs to be expanded upward to include help for the middle-income family—in many ways the most frustrated in its hope to send its youngsters to college because of the very little financial assistance available. Keep in mind that the degree to which attending a given college is financially out of reach makes no difference to the end result—the youngster from the family with a $16,000 income (who might have five brothers and sisters) is no less excluded from the educational opportunity than the student from a family with only a $6,000 income.

We have a situation here that presents a very special problem for the private college and university. As you've read on these pages and as many of us in the private sector have been warning for some time, private colleges and universities are becoming schools for the very rich and for the needy, who, thank God, in recent years have been able to reach out for assistance from a variety of private and public sources. But there are thousands of middle-income families who are interested in private higher education and there are hundreds of private institutions interested in them.

Hence the Federal government should have two fundamental objectives in expanding student aid (especially the education opportunity and work-study grants): First, to give all Americans a better opportunity to choose among all of the colleges and universities in the country; second, to initiate incentives for the states to improve their own student aid programs (as covered on previous pages).

The Senate and House bills vary somewhat in their approach to student grants. Lest what I have said so far indicates a bias towards the House of Representatives, I should point out that there are certain innovations contained in the Senate bill with regard to education opportunity grants which are worthy of passage. The education opportunity grants make available monies to students from financially disadvantaged families. While the House version increases the maximum payment from $1,000 to $1,500, the Senate under its new concept of "entitlement" would grant a total up to $1,400 maximum, minus an "expected family contribution." Under the Senate bill the grant could not amount to more than 50 percent of the actual cost at the particular institution. The innovations contained in the Senate bill include supplementary grants up to $1,200 for students who find that the basic grant is insufficient or for students whose family contributions render them ineligible for the basic grant.

I am especially pleased with the previously mentioned state scholarship incentive which, under the Senate version, authorizes $50 million through fiscal 1975 to match state grants to students on an even basis.

In the area of work-study grants, the Senate version contains a provision of which I heartily approve. This provision calls for considering the cost of attending the institution in determining a student's need for work.

STUDENT LOANS. As stated earlier in Section III, the usefulness and desirability of loans has been exaggerated. However, I did not want to give the impression that I do not see loans as both a continuing and necessary element in the financing of a student's higher education.

The two proposed bills also vary somewhat in their approach to student loans. With regard to the National Defense Student Loan (NDSL) provisions, the House version adopts the Educational Opportunity Grant formula for allocations among states as well as setting loan ceilings for graduate and professional students, for B.A. students at $5,000 and other students at $2,500.

Both the House and Senate versions increase the guaranteed student loan ceilings from $1,500 to $2,500 annually and the House version increases the aggregate amount from $7,500 to $10,000. The Senate version limits loans to a prior borrower. The House version allows the institution, within Federal guidelines, to determine need.

The Emergency Student Loan provisions are basically the same in each version.

It was mentioned earlier that labor leaders participating in SEARCH discussions took a very dim view of the loan approach because of the dimension of the financial burden it imposes on the student. A girl whose education was underwritten by a loan would bring a "negative dowry" to her marriage. Young newlyweds, both carrying such indebtedness, would be saddled with a seemingly interminable task just to someday pay off the costs of their education. Such a burden would lead almost inevitably to a decline in alumni giving.

For the average student, then, a loan system must remain no more than supplementary to all the other means of financing students and institutions. In that regard, because of the diversity that characterizes our institutions and our students, their backgrounds, and needs, it is unlikely that any one single method for financing higher education ever will be adequate or desirable.

CATEGORICAL GRANTS.   Little really need be said about a third type of Federal aid to higher education which actually is the oldest and best established—the myriad programs generally designated as categorical in nature: research grants, graduate fellowships, traineeships and so forth. It is through these channels that the federal government meets some of the current and/or continuing national needs, interests or crises which ordinary resources simply cannot meet or which are so specialized and extensive that the objective can only be achieved at the national level. Hopefully any new program of aid, such as general institutional grants and increased student subsidy, will not cause the important contract grant programs to be diminished or less fully funded. Graduate and professional aspects of our higher education which depend heavily on this source of assistance must not be allowed to deteriorate.

part seven

WHERE TO FROM HERE?

My intention, as stated at the outset, has been to write this report as a summary of my discussions held across the country under the auspices of Project SEARCH. The objective was to determine what should be done immediately at the institutional, state, and Federal level if we as a nation are truly in favor of preserving a pluralistic framework for higher education. I trust that my recommendations thus far, if not world-shaking, are at least clear and reasonable. However, the SEARCH experience has brought me to another conclusion which I offer not as a remedy that could have immediate effects but as a development which should be carefully explored and initiated immediately. It may turn out ten years from now that the health and strength of our total higher educational system may have been determined by the realization of such a proposal.

By way of preface and as background for the reader outside the educational community, the field of postsecondary education is represented in Washington by a plethora of associations.

The American Council on Education is the umbrella association with practically all colleges and universities as institutional members and nearly all of the associations and organizations interested in higher education as constituent members.

Then there is an association for almost every imaginable interest group: the Association of American Colleges (with special interest in undergraduate liberal arts education), the Association of American Universities (a group of more than 70 self-designated, prestigious institutions), the National Council of Independent Colleges and Universities, and many others. All of these organizations have heavily overlapping institutional memberships which means that hard pressed budgets are paying annual dues to sometimes 100 or more associations along with travel and living expenses to attend annual or more frequent meetings.

The Washington Secretariat is composed of the staff officers of the above mentioned American Council on Education, Association of American Colleges and Association of American Universities as well as the National Association of State Universities and Land Grant Colleges, the American Association of State Colleges and Universities, the Council for the Advancement of Small Colleges, the College and University Department of the National Catholic Educational Association, the American Association of Colleges for Teacher Education, the Council of Graduate Schools in the United States, the Association of Governing Boards of Universities and Colleges, the National Commission on Accrediting, the American Association of University Professors, and the American Association for Higher Education. The Secretariat recently commissioned a study to be carried out by Harland G. Bloland and O. Meredith Wilson. The study was to aid them in determining what steps should be taken towards closer cooperation and possible consolidation and, therefore, included a charge to investigate objectives, structures, overlap and duplication, bases for cooperation, member knowledgeability about other member associations. While the study to date has provided some interesting historical background, its recommendations, to me at least, leave something to be desired. Basically, the study recommends that the member associations be given representation on the ACE's Board of Directors and that in keeping with the new makeup of the Board a constituent assembly be created which would be composed of representatives of all the Council's constituent organization members. Eight members of the Board of

Directors of the ACE would be designated association representatives and would be chosen by this constituent assembly. Personally I would judge that the Bloland-Wilson recommendations do not go far enough.

During my 30 years in higher education (including 23 as a university president), I have often heard and participated in the argument that the entire educational scheme in Washington needs revamping insofar as representation and operations are concerned. It is generally regarded as excessively duplicative if not downright self-competitive. As such, it is costing higher education dollars we cannot afford to spend, not to mention the waste of time and effort on the part of hundreds of talented people working in either staff or voluntary capacities. (Please bear in mind that I am referring here only to the private educational organizations and not the equally numerous and complex offices and agencies within the Federal government which concern themselves with higher education, e.g., the U.S. Office of Education.)

Towards a Unifying Voice

In view of the foregoing, my proposal is that a neutral and mutually agreed upon task force be appointed to study and conceive a plan for major consolidation of our academic community in Washington. And the main reason for my thinking is not only the obvious projected savings in manpower, time, and money but also the critical need for more unified positions regarding basic matters of national educational policy, no matter how diverse and individualistic our separate organizations might be otherwise.

But even more unified positions are not enough. We have to unite, not merely to determine what our common voice will say, but also—and this is more difficult—to determine *how* we are going to say it in such a way that we are heard and listened to by Congress, the Administration and the public at large.

I believe it would be unwise at this point to propose a specific method by which higher education could more rapidly achieve such an end. A number of preparatory steps would have to be taken. The major associations would have to agree that they are in sympathy with the goal, though it may lead to some loss of autonomy and visibility or individual recognition. Then they would have to participate in planning such a consolidation. Sources of support, particularly the major foundations, would have to be convinced that this might be one of the greatest contributions an interested party could make in behalf of higher education and hence be persuaded to appropriate funds for implementation of the consolidation study and planning.

Also, continuing expert advice would have to be sought from leaders in other fields who know from experience how other national interest groups are organized to carry out their common objectives with effective unity and without losing a significant amount of their local autonomy. Surely the gain would far overbalance any sacrifices involved. It would seem that the question to be answered is whether we of the educational community have the mutual trust and respect to work out, among all of our diversified institutions and our variety of national organizations, a structure that will accommodate us all and engender a harmony of purpose at the national level so that our activities are coordinated, so that we are consistent when presenting our needs and so that we achieve the impact that fragmented and cross-purpose efforts cannot have.

Only by uniting will the sundry increments of higher education's Washington presence ever form a compelling enough entity to win for it a deserved high ranking among national priorities. We are coming to understand at long last that the United States, though still a land of plenty, has finite, limited resources. Higher education must compete in a very real sense for the same dollars as does ecology, agricultural aid, health care, highway construction, defense, and hundreds of other causes. Shall we enter such competition as individual droplets—the association of such-and-such colleges versus foreign aid needs—or as a single imposing tide, the prevailing voice of American higher education?

A Few Last Words

To conclude, the answer to the question, who needs private higher education is clear. We all do. We have seen that the quality of overall American higher education could diminish without the healthy competition and the potential for innovation and variety of style provided by our private sector.

To this we can add the economic case for the private sector which provides higher education for a sizable portion of our populace—including faculty and facilities—which otherwise would have to be supplied by a public system already burdened to the limit, and at a considerable additional cost to taxpayers.

Clearly our independent colleges and universities benefit not only higher education but society at large, serving our economic as well as our social best interests.

But to restore and strengthen the private sector of higher education in our land will require deliberate effort. Spearheading that effort as these pages are being written are the private institutions themselves, and rightly so. Their task is all too clearly defined. Each of our independent colleges and universities must decide what its essential mission is and then pursue it. In this way we will again exert influence over our own destiny, irrespective of economic constraints. We cannot drift. We must break down calcified habits and eliminate those programs and functions that continue on sheer bureaucratic momentum. Our pruning must be deft, if not merciless, as we reshape for tomorrow—or tomorrow will not come.

We must fuse academic excellence with stringent fiscal responsibility, yet economics must not fix the character of our higher education process. Likewise we must not harbor a mistaken conception of efficiency—it is not automatically a virtue, nor is it automatically desirable. Public support for efficiencies within higher education should depend upon the relevance of these efficiencies to the quality of the educational experience and not solely upon their budget balancing potential.

We must welcome change, yet never should change on our

campuses be a matter of panicky swings of direction, a welter of confused responses to demands and criticism. Rather, change must be a carefully-thought-through development adopted with regard for continuity as well. Moreover, we need not seek to change dramatically or even greatly overnight. For often major change comes about through a succession of small innovations. What is important is that we be responsive to the new needs and conditions of our society, that we be receptive to proposals for change within our institutions, and that we encourage new ways of doing things. But never should we allow ourselves to adopt the new, or to embrace the innovative without having required that it suit the goals that we have set.

It might well be said of America's private higher education that its achievements have been Homeric, its agonies have become Sophoclean and that its prospects resemble the Perils of Pauline. Overmatched against the arch-villain inflation, in concert with, lessening support (both financial and attitudinal), and demands from all directions . . . the system of independent colleges and universities, which today educates one-fourth of our young, may topple. Some experts predict it will.

Not, however, if we as private citizens, as students and as parents . . . as voters and taxpayers . . . as members of state and Federal governments . . . as alumni and as educators . . . as corporate and foundation supporters—in other words if we as a responsible society—will it otherwise.

To understand and to care is what is involved. And to the extent that Project SEARCH furthers that understanding and deepens that concern, its purpose is achieved.

ABOUT THE AUTHOR

THE REVEREND PAUL C. REINERT, S.J.
Project Director, SEARCH
President, Saint Louis University

The Rev. Paul C. Reinert, S.J., has earned a national reputation as an outstanding educator, citizen and intellectual. He has been president of Saint Louis University for 23 years at this writing.

The high regard of other educators for Father Reinert's leadership is reflected in the number of offices he has held in educational groups. He has been president of the Association of Urban Universities, the College and University Department of the National Catholic Educational Association, the North Central Association of Colleges and Secondary Schools and the Missouri Association of Colleges and Universities. He is the 1972 chairman of the Association of American Colleges. He is or has been a member of the board of directors of the American Council on Education, the National Catholic Educational Association, the Council for Financial Aid to Education, the Midwest Research Institute and the Educational Testing Service of Princeton, N.J.

Father Reinert also is respected as an active civic leader of

St. Louis. In 1963 he was named "Man of the Year" by the *St. Louis Globe Democrat.* In this recognition of his contribution to the city, he was cited for "services to the community, state, and nation which were above and beyond the call of duty." He served as co-chairman of the Mayor's Commission on Equal Employment Opportunities during the crucial years 1963–1965. He has served on the Citizens' Job Opportunity Commission and was a member of the board of directors of the St. Louis Civic Alliance for Housing. He is a dedicated member of Civic Progress, Inc., a small group of St. Louis leaders who have guided the redevelopment of the city. He was a leader in bringing an educational TV station to the city and serves on its advisory council.

Father Reinert has served on a number of Federal commissions in the U.S. Department of Health, Education, and Welfare and the Department of Defense. He was a member of the Danforth Commission on Church Colleges and Universities which made one of the most thorough and widely discussed studies of church-related colleges and universities in a number of years.

He earned two degrees at Saint Louis University and a Ph.D. in education administration from the University of Chicago. He has been awarded honorary degrees by 15 colleges and universities. He was appointed dean of the College of Arts and Sciences of Saint Louis University in 1944, academic vice-president in 1948 and president in 1949. His most recent publication is "The Urban Catholic University" issued in 1970.

Under Father Reinert's vigorous and farsighted leadership, Saint Louis University has become an institution of national stature and a partner in the rebirth of St. Louis. The university has an enrollment of approximately 11,000 and a faculty numbering nearly 2,000.

A strong stamp of approval of the university's strides "toward a destiny of distinction" was the receipt of a $5,000,000 Ford Foundation Challenge Grant in 1965. Only 15 other universities had received grants under the Special Education Program. The schools were selected on the basis of their superior scholarship and demonstrated potential for development as "regional and national centers of excellence."

ABOUT THE AUTHOR

Because of Father Reinert's efforts, Saint Louis University, in 1967, became the first major Catholic university to give laymen and clergy combined legal responsibility for institutional policy and operations.

He is now leading the university in an intensive restructuring of its curricular and fiscal programs. The study is called "Project 21: A Redesign of the University for the 21st Century." It is supported by a $1,500,000 grant from the Danforth Foundation.